CONTENTS

How to Use This Book

THE AUTHOR AND HIS TIMES 1

THE NOVEL 11

The Plot 11

The Characters 17

Other Elements 27

- Setting 27
- Themes 28
- Style 31
- Point of Vi 32
- Form and 4

The Story 7

A STEP BEYON 9

Tests and Answers 79

Term Paper Ideas 88

Further Reading 93

- Critical Works 93
- Author's Other Works 95

Glossary 96

The Critics 99

W0400557

HOW TO USE THIS BOOK

You have to know how to approach literature in order to get the most out of it. This *Barron's Book Notes* volume follows a plan based on methods used by some of the best students to read a work of literature.

Begin with the guide's section on the author's life and times. As you read, try to form a clear picture of the author's personality, circumstances, and motives for writing the work. This background usually will make it easier for you to hear the author's tone of voice, and follow where the author is heading.

Then go over the rest of the introductory material—such sections as those on the plot, characters, setting, themes, and style of the work. Underline, or write down in your notebook, particular things to watch for, such as contrasts between characters and repeated literary devices. At this point, you may want to develop a system of symbols to use in marking your text as you read. (Of course, you should only mark up a book you own, not one that belongs to another person or a school.) Perhaps you will want to use a different letter for each character's name, a different number for each major theme of the book, a different color for each important symbol or literary device. Be prepared to mark up the pages of your book as you read. Put your marks in the margins so you can find them again easily.

Now comes the moment you've been waiting for—the time to start reading the work of literature. You may want to put aside your *Barron's Book Notes* volume until you've read the work all the way through. Or you may want to alternate, reading the *Book Notes* analysis of each section as soon as you have finished reading the corresponding part of the original. Before you move on, reread crucial passages you don't fully understand. (Don't take this guide's analysis for granted—make up your own mind as to what the work means.)

Once you've finished the whole work of literature, you may want to review it right away, so you can firm up your ideas about what it means. You may want to leaf through the book concentrating on passages you marked in reference to one character or one theme. This is also a good time to reread the *Book Notes* introductory material, which pulls together insights on specific topics.

When it comes time to prepare for a test or to write a paper, you'll already have formed ideas about the work. You'll be able to go back through it, refreshing your memory as to the author's exact words and perspective, so that you can support your opinions with evidence drawn straight from the work. Patterns will emerge, and ideas will fall into place; your essay question or term paper will almost write itself. Give yourself a dry run with one of the sample tests in the guide. These tests present both multiple-choice and essay questions. An accompanying section gives answers to the multiple-choice questions as well as suggestions for writing the essays. If you have to select a term paper topic, you may choose one from the list of suggestions in this book. This guide also provides you with a reading list, to help you when you start research for a term paper, and a selection of provocative comments by critics, to spark your thinking before you write.

THE AUTHOR AND HIS TIMES

Have you ever felt that there were two of you battling for control of the person you call yourself? Have you ever felt that you weren't quite sure which one you wanted to be in charge? All of us have at least two selves: one who wants to work hard, get good grades, and be successful; and one who would rather lie in the sun and listen to music and daydream. To understand F. Scott Fitzgerald, the man and the writer, you must begin with the idea of *doubleness,* or *twoness.*

Fitzgerald himself said in a famous series of essays called *The Crack Up,* "the test of a first-rate intelligence is the ability to hold two opposed ideas in the mind at the same time, and still retain the ability to function." Everything about Fitzgerald is touched by this idea. For example, he both loved and hated money. He was attracted to the life of the very rich as an outsider who had very little, and at the same time he hated the falseness and hypocrisy and cruelty of their lives. He was disciplined, knowing that he had to have great mental and physical self-control to succeed as a writer; but he was often unable to exercise those very qualities he knew he would need in order to succeed. He loved his wife Zelda more than anything in his life, and yet he hated her for destroying his talent. Part of him lived a dazzling life full of parties, gaiety, and show; and part of him knew that this sort of life was a complete sham.

All of this doubleness Fitzgerald puts into the novel you are about to read: *The Great Gatsby.* As you begin reading think about Nick Carraway, the narrator of the novel, and Jay Gatsby, the hero of the novel, as the two sides of Fitzgerald. Think of Fitzgerald as putting into his two main characters both of the people that he knew he had within him. As you read, ask yourself whether or not you have these two people within you: Nick, the intelligent and disciplined observer; and Gatsby, the passionate and idealistic dreamer who wants his dream so much that he will sacrifice everything for it.

Fitzgerald himself seemed genetically destined for doubleness. His mother's father, P. F. McQuillan, went to St. Paul, Minnesota, in 1857, at the age of twenty-three. In twenty years he built up—literally from nothing—an enormously successful wholesale business. He was a totally self-made man, and from him Scott inherited a sense of self-reliance and a belief in hard work. The Fitzgeralds, on the other hand, were an old Maryland family. Scott himself—Francis Scott Key Fitzgerald was his full name—was named for his great, great, great grandfather's brother, the man who wrote "The Star Spangled Banner." And Edward Fitzgerald, Scott's father, was a handsome, charming man, but one who seemed more interested in the family name than in hard work.

The McQuillan and the Fitzgerald in Scott vied for control throughout his childhood. He was a precocious child, full of energy and imagination, but he liked to take short cuts, substituting flights of fantasy for hard work. On his seventh birthday in 1903 he told a number of the older guests that he was the owner of a yacht (perhaps the seeds of Gatsby's admiration for Dan Cody's yacht in the novel). As an adolescent he loved to play theatrical games—pretending to be drunk on a streetcar or telephoning an artificial limb company to discuss being fitted for a false limb. He was an excellent writer and a vivid satirist of his classmates, but his marks were not good; so, like so many Midwestern boys, he was shipped East to boarding school, where he would be taught discipline and hard work.

In September of 1911, with the words and music of Irving Berlin's new song "Alexander's Ragtime Band" uppermost on his mind, he enrolled at the Newman School in Hackensack, New Jersey, a popular Roman Catholic school among Midwestern families. Here he was to have two years to ready himself for a good Ivy League College, preferably Princeton or Yale. Scott chose Princeton, but Princeton very nearly didn't choose him.

The doubleness in Scott is beautifully illustrated by the way in which he maneuvered himself into Princeton. An avid writer and reader, Fitzgerald tended to read what he liked and ignore his school work, and therefore he failed his entrance exams during his senior year. After a "summer of study," he took them again and failed them again. Finally on September 24, 1913, his seventeenth birthday, he appeared before the Admissions Committee and convinced them to accept him. Personal magnetism was able to achieve what hard work had not.

One of the things Scott inherited from his Grandfather McQuillan was ambition. Scott was a fierce competitor, and if he wanted something badly enough he could work like a demon. What Scott wanted were women and popularity, and the way to win women and be popular, he had learned at Newman, was with money, good looks, and athletics. He didn't have the first, but he had the second, and he worked very, very hard at the third by trying out for freshman football. His problem was that he was only 5'6" and weighed only 130 pounds, which doesn't get one very far in football. So he scrapped the football pads and found another outlet for his energy and his ambition: writing musical comedies. One of the most prestigious organizations at Princeton was and still is the Triangle Club, a group that writes and produces a musical comedy every year. (Among its graduates are the actors Jimmy Stewart and Jose Ferrer.)

Fitzgerald devoted most of his energies at Princeton to the Triangle Show, writing the book and lyrics in his freshman year and the lyrics in his sophomore year. He was elected secretary of the club, and was in line to become its president—something he wanted more than anything in his life. But it was not to be. In December of 1915, the fall of his junior year, he was sent home with malaria. He was told when he returned in March that he would have to fall back a year and that he was academically ineligible for the Triangle presidency. In the spring of 1917 his class graduated, and Scott was left behind to complete his senior year. He never did; instead, he enlisted in the army.

Why? Perhaps because he wanted to be a hero, and the United States was about to make the world safe for democracy. Perhaps because college was no fun anymore. Perhaps because beautiful women love young men in uniform. Whatever the reason, Fitzgerald left Princeton in November and found himself in the summer of 1918 stationed at Camp Sheridan, outside Montgomery, Alabama. Here 2nd Lieutenant Scott Fitzgerald met Miss Zelda Sayre, who was to become his wife and the single most important influence on his life. Zelda was seventeen, and a combination of tomboy and Southern belle. She was used to having her own way with her traditional parents, and she very much enjoyed being courted by the officers from Camp Sheridan, just as Daisy in *The Great Gatsby* is courted by the young officers at Camp Taylor.

It was love at first sight. Just as Jay Gatsby, an outsider with no money and no respectable family, falls utterly in love with Daisy Fay, so the Midwestern outsider Scott Fitzgerald fell head over heels in love with the Montgomery belle Zelda Sayre. He loved her beauty, her daring, her originality. He loved her crazy, romantic streak which matched his own. He proposed to her, and she turned him down. Like Jay Gatsby, he was too young and he had no money, and she could not be sure he would ever amount to anything.

So he went off to war but, unlike Gatsby, he never got to Europe. By the time his regiment had been sent overseas, the Armistice had been signed and his dreams of military glory had to be set aside with the football pads and the presidency of the Triangle Club. But Scott was determined to be famous, and in March of 1919— this time like Nick Carraway—he went to New York to learn his trade. Scott's trade was writing and he had written, during his long, lonely months in the army, a novel about life at boarding school and at Princeton. But no one would publish it and Zelda, who had finally promised to marry him, changed her mind. In what he called his "long summer of despair," he went home to St. Paul, rewrote his novel, and submitted it to Charles Scribner's Sons. Maxwell Perkins, a young editor who was to become Fitzgerald's friend and supporter for life, accepted the book. In March of 1920, Scott Fitzgerald's first novel, *This Side of Paradise,* was published.

This Side of Paradise made Fitzgerald famous. It also made Zelda change her mind again. On April 3, 1920, in the Rectory of St. Patrick's Cathedral in New York City, they were married. Within two years they became the most notorious young couple in America, symbolizing what Fitzgerald called The Jazz Age.

The Jazz Age began, Fitzgerald tells us in his short story "May Day," in May of 1918. It ended with the stock market crash of 1929. The Jazz Age brought about one of the most rapid and pervasive changes in manners and morals the world has ever seen, changes that we are still wrestling with today. It was a period when the younger generation—men and women alike—were rebelling against the values and customs of their parents and grandparents. After all, the older generation had led thousands of young men into the most brutal and senseless war in human history. People of Fitzgerald's age had seen death, and when they came back, they were determined to have a good time. "How you gonna keep 'em down on the farm, now that they've seen Paree" was one of the most popular songs of the day.

And have a good time they did. The saxophone replaced the violin; skirt hemlines went up; corsets came off; women started smoking; and Prohibition, which was supposed to stop drinking, only reshaped it into secret fun. The public saloon, now illegal, was replaced by the private cocktail party, and men and women began drinking together. Parties like the ones given by Gatsby began to thrive, and hoodlums became millionaires in a few months by controlling the bootleg liquor business.

Scott and Zelda not only chronicled the age, they lived it. They rode down Fifth Avenue on the tops of taxis; they dove into the fountain in front of New York's famous Plaza Hotel. Scott fought with waiters, and Zelda danced on tabletops. They drank too much and passed out in corners; they drove recklessly and gave weekend parties, which were not too different from the ones Gatsby gives in the novel and which lasted until the small hours of Monday morning.

In the midst of all this, Fitzgerald tried to write. Part of him believed in work and tried repeatedly to discipline himself, to go "on the wagon," to give up parties.

Many years later in a beautiful letter to his daughter Scottie, he talked about the tension of those years: "When I was your age I lived with a great dream. The dream grew and I learned to speak of it and make people listen. Then the dream divided one day when I decided to marry your mother . . . I was a man divided—she wanted me to work too much for *her* and not enough for my dream."

The dream, of course, was his dream of being a great writer. *This Side of Paradise* had made him famous because it was the first novel that honestly described the life-style of the new generation, but his work during the first three years of his marriage was not nearly what he knew it could have been, and so in 1923 he set out to write a book that he could be proud of. In July 1923, Zelda wrote a friend: "Scott has started a new novel and retired into strict seclusion and celibacy." The new novel of course was *The Great Gatsby,* and the ten months he devoted to that novel was artistically the most disciplined ten months of his life. The novel was published in the spring of 1925. Though sales were disappointing, the criticism was very positive. Great writers like the novelist Edith Wharton and the poet T. S. Eliot wrote Fitzgerald letters of congratulations. And Gertrude Stein, who called Fitzgerald and Ernest Hemingway members of a "lost generation," gave great praise to the book. Hemingway himself, a new friend of Fitzgerald's in 1925, loved *The Great Gatsby.*

Fitzgerald was never again to reach the success of *Gatsby*. Until 1925 the Nick Carraway in him had sustained him enough to keep him writing well, but just as Gatsby's love for Daisy drove him to tragedy, so Fitzgerald's love for Zelda occupied more and more of his time. To maintain the social style she loved, he wrote stories for the popular magazines of the time, like *Cosmopolitan*, *Smart Set*, and the *Saturday Evening Post*. Maintaining a dizzying social life, Scott, Zelda, and their daughter Scottie moved from New York City to Great Neck, Long Island (the model for West Egg in *Gatsby*), eventually on to Paris and the Riviera, and finally back to the United States. He could not finish another novel, and he could not make Zelda happy. She became more and more depressed, and finally in April 1930, Zelda had a complete breakdown and had to be hospitalized.

The great stock market crash of 1929 had ended America's decade of prosperity, and Zelda's breakdown in 1930 ended the Fitzgerald's decade as the symbol of The Jazz Age. The party was over.

From 1930 until his death in Hollywood in 1940, Scott struggled to regain the stature he had earned with *The Great Gatsby*, but he never could. He wrote *Tender is the Night*, which is a beautiful novel, during the early '30s, but when the book was published in 1934, America was not interested in a story about rich Americans partying on the French Riviera. This was the Depression, and the novelists in demand were Sherwood Anderson and John Steinbeck, writers who talked about the plight of poor people. Scott continued to care for Zelda, who was to spend the rest of her life in and out of sanitariums. He also kept writing. But during 1935 and 1936 he had his own breakdown, which he recorded brilliantly in the series of essays for *Esquire* called "The Crack Up."

Desperate for money, he took a job as a script writer for M-G-M in 1937, where he worked on and off for the next two years. With the support of his friend the columnist Sheilah Graham, in 1939 he began a new novel. Called *The Last Tycoon,* this book was based on the career of the legendary Hollywood producer Irving Thalberg, whom Fitzgerald greatly admired. But Fitzgerald's years of dissipation caught up with him, and he died of a heart attack on December 21, 1940. Even unfinished, *The Last Tycoon* is a fine novel, almost as good as *Gatsby*. But for a long time the world didn't know that. At the time of his death all of Fitzgerald's books were out of print. Scott who? Oh, that guy that used to write about the '20s.

Well, he was much more than that, and during the 1950s and 1960s people started reading Scott Fitzgerald again. Today he is considered one of America's great novelists. *The Great Gatsby,* along with *The Scarlet Letter* and *Huckleberry Finn,* has become a book we can't do without if we want to understand ourselves. Fitzgerald asks us to read this book with that same double vision with which he wrote it. He asks us to participate emotionally in the lives of its characters, especially Gatsby. And he asks us to stand back from them as Nick does and see what is wrong with them. He asks us to love and to evaluate at the same time, perhaps in the say way that Nick both loves and criticizes Gatsby.

THE NOVEL

The Plot

Nick Carraway, the narrator, is a young Midwesterner who, having graduated from Yale in 1915 and fought in World War I ("the Great War"), has returned home to begin a career. Like others in his generation, he is restless and has decided to move East to New York and learn the bond business. The novel opens early in the summer of 1922 in West Egg, Long Island, where Nick has rented a house. Next to his place is a huge mansion complete with Gothic tower and marble swimming pool, which belongs to a Mr. Gatsby, whom Nick has not met.

Directly across the bay from West Egg is the more fashionable community of East Egg, where Tom and Daisy Buchanan live. Daisy is Nick's cousin, and Tom, a well-known football player at Yale, had been in the same senior society as Nick in New Haven. Like Nick, they are Midwesterners who have come East to be a part of the glamour and mystery of the New York City area. They invite Nick to dinner at their mansion, and here he meets a young woman golfer named Jordan Baker, a friend of Daisy's from Louisville, whom Daisy wants Nick to become interested in.

During dinner the phone rings, and when Tom and Daisy leave the room, Jordan informs Nick that the caller is a "woman of Tom's from New York."

The woman's name is Myrtle Wilson, and she lives in a strange, fantastic place half way between West Egg and New York City that Fitzgerald calls the "valley of ashes." The valley of ashes consists of huge ash heaps and a faded yellow brick building containing an all-night restaurant and George Wilson's garage. Painted on a large billboard nearby is a fading advertisement for an optician: the eyes of Dr. T.J. Eckleburg, gazing out over this wasteland through a pair of enormous yellow spectacles.

One day Tom takes Nick to meet the Wilsons. Myrtle joins them on the next train to Manhattan, and the threesome ends up, along with a dog Myrtle buys at Pennsylvania Station, at the apartment Tom has rented for his meetings with Myrtle. Myrtle's sister Catherine and an unattractive couple from downstairs named McKee join them, and the six proceed to get quite drunk. The party breaks up violently when Myrtle starts using Daisy's name in a familiar fashion and Tom, in response, breaks her nose with a blow of his open hand.

Some weeks later Nick finally gets the opportunity to meet his mysterious neighbor Mr. Gatsby. Gatsby gives huge parties, complete with catered food, open bars, and orchestras. People come from everywhere to attend these parties, but no one seems to know much about the host. Legends about Jay Gatsby abound. Some say he was a German spy during the war, others, that he once killed a man. Nick becomes fascinated by Gatsby. He begins watching his host and notices that Gatsby does not drink or join in the revelry of his own parties.

One day Gatsby and Nick drive to New York together. Gatsby tells Nick that he's from a wealthy family in the Midwest, that he was educated at Oxford, and that he won war medals from many European countries. Nick isn't sure what to believe. At lunch Gatsby introduces Nick to his business associate, Meyer Wolfsheim, "the man who fixed the World Series in 1919."

At tea that afternoon Nick finds out from Jordan Baker why Gatsby has taken such an interest in him: Gatsby is in love with Daisy Buchanan and wants Nick to arrange a meeting between them. It seems that Gatsby, as a young officer at Camp Taylor in 1917, had fallen in love with Daisy, then Daisy Fay. He had been sent overseas, and she had eventually given him up, married Tom Buchanan, and had a daughter. When Gatsby finally returned from Europe he decided to win Daisy back. His first step was to buy a house in West Egg. From here he could look across the bay to the green light at the end of Daisy's dock. He expected her to turn up at one of his parties, and when she didn't, he asked Jordan to ask Nick to ask Daisy. And so Nick does.

A few days later, in the rain, Gatsby and Daisy meet for the first time in five years. Gatsby is at first terrified, then tremendously excited. He takes Nick and Daisy on a tour of his house and grounds and shows them all his possessions, even his beautiful shirts from England. He shows Daisy the green light that he has been watching, and he insists that Klipspringer, "the boarder," play the piano for them. Klipspringer plays "Ain't We Got Fun," and Nick leaves.

Now, halfway through the book, Nick gives us some information about who Gatsby really is. He was originally James Gatz, the son of farm people from North Dakota. He had gone to St. Olaf College in Minnesota, dropped out because the college failed to promote his romantic dreams about himself, and ended up on the south shore of Lake Superior earning room and board by digging clams and fishing for salmon. One day he saw the beautiful yacht of the millionaire Dan Cody and borrowed a rowboat to warn Cody of an impending storm. Cody took the seventeen-year-old boy on as steward, mate, and secretary. When Cody died, he left the boy, now Jay Gatsby, a legacy of $25,000, which the boy never got because of the jealousy of Cody's mistress.

The story of Gatsby's past breaks off, and Nick resumes his narration of Gatsby's renewed courtship of Daisy during the summer of 1922. Daisy and Tom come to one of Gatsby's parties, but Tom is put off by the vulgarity of Gatsby's world, and Daisy does not have a good time. Though Gatsby has been seeing Daisy, he's increasingly frustrated by his inability to recreate the magic of their time together in Louisville five years before.

The affair between Daisy and Gatsby now comes out into the open. Tom, Daisy, Gatsby, Nick, and Jordan—the five major characters—all meet for lunch at the Buchanans and then decide to drive to New York. Daisy and Gatsby end up going together in the Buchanans' blue coupe; Tom, Nick, and Jordan drive in Gatsby's yellow Rolls Royce. The couple stop for gas at Wilson's garage, and Myrtle Wilson, watching from her window over the garage, thinks the car belongs to Tom.

The five arrive in the city and engage the parlor of a suite at the Plaza Hotel. Tom, drunk and agitated by now, starts ragging Gatsby about his past and attacking him for his phony English habit of calling people "old sport." Gatsby retaliates by telling Tom that Daisy is going to leave him. Tom calls Gatsby a cheap bootlegger. Like cowboys in the Old West, they duel back and forth for Daisy until Tom wins. Daisy will not go away with Gatsby, and the five-year dream is over. Tom sends Daisy and Gatsby home together in the yellow Rolls Royce, knowing that he has nothing more to fear. A couple of hours later Tom follows with

Nick and Jordan. When they reach the valley of ashes, they see crowds of people and police cars. Someone was struck by a car coming from New York. That someone, they discover, was Myrtle Wilson, and the car had to be Gatsby's yellow Rolls Royce. When Nick gets back to East Egg, he finds Gatsby hiding in the shrubbery outside the Buchanans' house, unwilling to leave for fear that Tom might hurt Daisy. Gatsby tells Nick that Daisy was driving, but that—of course—he will take the blame. Nick leaves Gatsby "watching over nothing."

Nick goes to work the next morning, but is too worried about Gatsby to stay in New York. He takes an early train back to West Egg but arrives at Gatsby's too late. His friend's body is floating on an inflated mattress in the swimming pool, and George Wilson's dead body, revolver in hand, lies nearby on the grass. The crazed husband had spent the entire morning tracking down the driver of the yellow Rolls Royce. He found Gatsby before Nick did.

Nick tries to phone Daisy and Tom, but is told they've left town with no forwarding address. Calls to Meyer Wolfsheim produce similar results. Nick, it seems, is Gatsby's only friend.

News of Gatsby's murder is printed in a Chicago newspaper, where it is read by his father, Mr. Henry C. Gatz, now of Minnesota. Mr. Gatz arrives for the funeral, which is attended only by Nick, Owl Eyes (who loved Gatsby's books), and a smattering of servants. Meyer Wolfsheim, of course, has refused to get involved. Even Mr. Klipspringer, "the boarder," has sent his excuses.

Mr. Gatz, who loves his son very much, shows Nick a book which Jimmy owned as a boy. In the flyleaf Gatsby had written a schedule for self improvement: exercise, study, sport, and work. How far Gatsby had come from that dream, to this meaningless death!

Disgusted and disillusioned by what he has experienced, Nick decides to leave New York and return to the Midwest. He ends his relationship with Jordan Baker and learns from Tom Buchanan that it was he, Tom, who told Wilson where Gatsby lived. Before Nick leaves the East, he stands one more time on the beach near Gatsby's house looking out at the green light that his friend had worshipped. Here he pays his final tribute to Gatsby and to the dream for which he lived—and died.

The Characters

Nick Carraway

Nick Carraway is the narrator of *The Great Gatsby;* he is also a character in the novel. When you think about him, you have to think about what Fitzgerald is using him for. You also have to look at him as a person.

Nick, is first of all, Fitzgerald's means of making his story more realistic. Because Nick is experiencing events and telling us about them in his own words, we're more likely to believe the story. After a while we almost begin to experience the events as Nick does; the *I* of each of us as readers replaces the *I* of Nick. (For more details, see "Point of View.")

Nick is a narrator whose values you should have no trouble identifying or at least sympathizing with. He's not mad or blind to what's going on around him. He's a pretty solid young man who has graduated from Yale University, served his country in the First World War, and decided to go into the bond business. He comes from a solid Midwestern family, from whom he has learned some pretty basic values. He is honest, but not Puritanical or narrow minded. He is tolerant, understanding, and not hasty to judge people. He is the sort of person you might talk to if you wanted a sympathetic ear. But his toleration has limits. He doesn't approve of everything.

These are some of the qualities that make Nick a reliable narrator, someone whose story we are likely to believe. It seems often that his values are pretty close to those of the author.

Nick is in a perfect position to tell the story. He is a cousin of Daisy Buchanan's, he was in the same senior society as Tom Buchanan at Yale, and he has rented, during the summer of 1922, a house right next to Jay Gatsby. He knows all the characters well enough to be present at the crucial scenes in the novel. The information he doesn't have but needs in order to tell his story, he gets from other characters like Jordan Baker, the Greek restaurant owner Michaelis, and Gatsby himself. Nick knows things because people confess to him, and people confess to him because he is tolerant, understanding and sympathetic.

Nick has that capacity, which Fitzgerald felt was so terribly important (see The Author and His Times), of holding two contradictory opinions at the same time. He both admires Gatsby and disapproves of him. He admires Gatsby both because of his dream and because of his basic *innocence;* and he disapproves of Gatsby for his vulgar materialism and his corrupt business practices. (Nick does not want to become involved with Meyer Wolfsheim, Gatsby's underworld "connection.")

One of the things that makes Nick special is that he understands Gatsby. Nobody else in the novel—not even Daisy—really understands him. Nick is, at the novel's end, Gatsby's only friend, even though he disapproves of many things which Gatsby stands for. Almost nobody comes to Gatsby's funeral, and if it weren't for Nick, there would probably not even have been a funeral. Would you have gone?

Some readers think Nick is too sympathetic to Gatsby. They think that Nick ought to be mature enough to see what is wrong with Gatsby's dream. They feel that Nick should be more critical of Gatsby, and force us as readers to be more critical, too. They believe that Nick, in the closing pages, is too sentimental and that his judgment is not as reliable as we might think. There's no critical agreement on this issue, so you'll have to make up your own minds as you read the book.

As you're deciding about Nick's powers of judgment—particularly in the opening and closing pages where he talks about himself—keep in mind that Nick is a Midwesterner and his values are colored by the values of the world in which he grew up.

Many readers have remarked that the novel is based on a contrast between the solid, traditional, conservative Midwest and the glamorous, glittering, fast-paced world of the East. Nick (like Scott Fitzgerald, his creator) is from Minnesota. He comes East to experience the new and exciting world of New York that is very different from Minneapolis–St. Paul. At the end, he chooses to leave the East and return to the Midwest. By that choice he seems to be saying to us that he has tried the East and found it missing something he needs: a basic set of values. So he goes home, where values still exist. Think about the two worlds—the Midwest and the East and what they represented for Nick (and by extension, Fitzgerald) and what they might represent for you.

Jay Gatsby

The title of this novel is *The Great Gatsby*. If you like paradoxes, start with this one: he is neither great nor Gatsby (his real name was Gatz). He is a crook, a bootlegger who has involved himself with Meyer Wolfsheim, the man who fixed the 1919 World Series. He has committed crimes in order to buy the house he feels he needs to win the woman he loves, who happens to be another man's wife. Thus a central question for us as readers is, why should we love such a man? Or, to put it in other word, what makes Gatsby great? Why, *despite* all these things, does Fitzgerald invite us to cry out with Nick, " 'They're a rotten crowd' . . . 'You're worth the whole damn bunch put together.' "?

We are asked to love Gatsby, even admire him to a point, because of his dream. That dream is what separates Gatsby from what Nick calls the "foul dust [that] floated in the wake of his dreams . . ." It is not merely what is known as the American Dream of Success—the belief that every man can rise to success no matter what his beginnings. It is a kind of romantic idealism, "some heightened sensitivity to the promises of life," Nick calls it. It is a belief in fairytales and princesses and happy endings, a faith that life can be special, remarkable, beautiful. Gatsby is not interested in power for its own sake or in money or prestige. What he wants is his dream, and that dream is embodied in Daisy. He must have her, and, as the novel's epigraph on the title page suggests, he will do anything that is required in order to win her.

But dreams don't always show on the outside. *The Great Gatsby* is a kind of mystery story with Gatsby as the mystery. Who is he? All the way through the novel people keep asking that question and answering it falsely. They answer it falsely because they aren't really interested in who Gatsby is. They have heard things about him—that he killed a man, that he was a German spy in World War I—and they pass these bits of gossip on to other people. So the myth of Gatsby—the collection of false stories about him—hides the Gatsby that we come gradually to know through the efforts of Nick Carraway. Nick genuinely cares who Gatsby is, and in Chapters IV, VI, VIII, and IX he presents us with the story of Gatsby's past as he has learned it from Jordan Baker, from Gatsby himself, and eventually, from Gatsby's father.

No one else but Nick knows or understands Gatsby's background except maybe his father and Owl Eyes—and they, significantly, are the only ones present at his funeral. Fitzgerald invites us to share Nick's understanding of Gatsby as we read the novel. He makes us see behind the surface of the man who at first glance looks like a young roughneck. And he forces us to ask, as we finish the book, what this dream is that Gatsby has dedicated himself to. Is it a worthwhile dream? Is it our dream, too? Can we love Gatsby and be critical of his dream at the same time? Fitzgerald makes us ask these questions and then lets us find our own answers.

Tom Buchanan

Tom Buchanan, Nick tells us, "had been one of the most powerful ends that ever played football at New Haven—a national figure in a way, one of those men who reach such an acute limited excellence at twenty-one that everything afterward savors of anticlimax." He is also very wealthy, having brought a string of polo ponies from Lake Forest to Long Island. This double power—the size of his body and his bankroll—colors our feelings about Tom Buchanan.

Because he is both very strong and very rich, Tom is used to having his own way. Nick describes him as having "a rather hard mouth" and "two shining arrogant eyes." When we first meet him in Chapter I, he reveals his crude belief in his own superiority by telling Nick that he has just read a book called *The Rise of the Colored Empires*. The book warns that if white people are not careful, the black races will rise up and overwhelm them. Tom clearly believes it.

Tom is having an affair with Myrtle Wilson, the wife of George Wilson, who runs a garage in the valley of ashes. Myrtle seems to have a dark sexual vitality that attracts Tom, and he keeps an apartment for her in New York, where he takes Nick in Chapter II. Here he again shows how little he thinks of anyone beside himself when he casually breaks Myrtle's nose with the back of his hand, because she is shouting "Daisy! Daisy!" in a vulgar fashion.

Between Chapters II and VII we see little of Tom, but in Chapter VII he emerges as a central figure. It is Tom who pushes the affair between Gatsby and Daisy out into the open by asking Gatsby point blank, " 'What kind of a row are you trying to cause in my house anyhow?' " It is Tom who verbally outduels Gatsby to win his wife back and deflate his rival's dream. And it is Tom who, after the death of Myrtle Wilson, tells George Wilson that Gatsby was the killer and then hustles Daisy out of the area until the affair blows over.

Fitzgerald describes Tom and Daisy as careless people who break things and then retreat into their wealth and let other people clean up their messes. It's a particularly apt metaphor for Tom, who cannot understand why Nick should have any ill feelings about Gatsby's death. After all, Tom was only protecting his wife. Nick shakes hands with Tom in the final chapter because ". . . I saw that what he had done was, to him, entirely justified." Yet Tom's behavior was not justifiable, and when Nick refers to the "foul dust" that floated in the wake of Gatsby's dream, he seems to be speaking of Tom Buchanan more than anyone else. It is Tom as much as anyone who sends Nick back to the Midwest, where there are still values one can believe in.

Daisy Fay Buchanan

She was born Daisy Fay in Louisville, Kentucky, and her color is white. When Jordan Baker, in Chapter IV, tells Nick about the first meeting between Gatsby and Daisy in October 1917, she says of Daisy, "She dressed in white, and had a little white roadster, and all day long the telephone rang in her house and excited young officers from Camp Taylor demanded the privilege of monopolizing her that night."

Throughout *The Great Gatsby* Daisy is described almost in fairytale language. The name *Fay* means "fairy" or "sprite." "Daisy," of course, suggests the flower, fresh and bright as spring, yet fragile and without the strength to resist the heat and dryness of summer.

Daisy is the princess in the tower, the golden girl that every man dreams of possessing. She is beautiful and rich and innocent and pure (at least on the surface) in her whiteness. But that whiteness, as you will notice, is mixed with the yellow of gold and the inevitable corruption that money brings. Though Daisy *seems* pure and white, she is a mixture of things, just like the flower for which she was named (see Schneider in "Critics").

Fitzgerald suggests the nature of this mixture beautifully in the famous passage from Chapter VII about her voice:

> "She's got an indiscreet voice," I remarked. "It's full of—" I hesitated.
>
> "Her voice is full of money," he said suddenly.
>
> That was it. I'd never understood it before. It was full of money—that was the inexhaustible charm that rose and fell in it, the jingle of it, the cymbals' song of it. . . . High in a white palace the king's daughter, the golden girl. . . .

Like money, Daisy promises more than she gives. Her voice seems to offer everything, but she's born to disappoint. She is the sort of person who is better to dream about than to actually possess. Fitzgerald—with that double vision we discussed in The Author and His Times section of this guide—knew very well both the attractions and the limitations of women like Daisy, who is modeled in many ways upon his wife Zelda.

Gatsby worships Daisy, and Nick distrusts her—just as Scott both worshipped and distrusted Zelda. Gatsby loves Daisy too much to see what is wrong with her. Nick stands back and sees the way Daisy lets other people take care of her in crises. If you want to study the nature of Daisy's weakness, look especially at her behavior on the night before her wedding and on the night of Myrtle Wilson's death. Daisy, unlike Tom, uses her money rather than her body or her personality to bully others. She uses her money to protect her from reality, and when reality threatens to hurt her, she cries and goes inside the protective womb her money has made.

Be careful not to identify Daisy with the green light at the end of her dock. The green light is the promise, the dream. Daisy herself is much less than that. Even Gatsby must realize that having Daisy in the flesh is much, much less than what he imagined it would be when he fell in love with the *idea* of her.

Jordan Baker

Jordan Baker's most striking quality is her dishonesty. She is tough and aggressive—a tournament golfer who is so hardened by competition that she is willing to do anything to win. At the end of Chapter IV, when Nick is telling us about Jordan, he remembers a story about her first major tournament. Apparently she moved her ball to improve her lie (!), but when the matter was being investigated, the caddy and the only other witness to the incident retracted their stories and nothing was proved against her. The incident should stay with you throughout the novel, reminding you (as it reminds Nick) that Jordan is the smart new woman, the opportunist who will do whatever she must to be successful in her world.

In many ways Jordan Baker symbolizes a new type of woman that was emerging in the Twenties. She is hard and self-sufficient, and she adopts whatever morals suit her situation. She has cut herself off from the older generation. She wears the kind of clothes that suit her; she smokes, she drinks, and has sex because she enjoys them. You may wish to explore Jordan as the new woman of the Twenties by looking at the manners and character traits she reveals. Note such things as her name (a masculine name), her body (hard, athletic, boyish, small-breasted), her style (blunt, cynical, bored), and her social background (she is cut off from past generations by having almost no family).

Another important aspect of Jordan is her function in the novel. Fitzgerald needs her to get the story told. Because she is Daisy's friend from Louisville, she can supply Nick with information he would not have otherwise. She also serves as a link between the major characters, moving back and forth between the world of East Egg (Tom and Daisy's house) and West Egg (Gatsby's and Nick's houses). She is rich enough to be comfortable among the East Eggers but enough of a social hustler to appear at Gatsby's parties.

Jordan serves still another purpose: Nick's girlfriend during the summer of 1922. The Nick-Jordan romance serves as a nice sub-plot to the Gatsby-Jordan relationship, and allows you to compare and contrast a romantic-idealistic love with a very practical relationship made on a temporary basis by two worldly people of the time.

If you want to explore the Nick-Jordan relationship and the possible reasons why Nick becomes involved with her and then breaks the relationship off, you'll need to look particularly at three passages: Nick's comments toward the end of Chapter III; the phone call between Nick and Jordan in Chapter VIII; and their final conversation in Chapter IX. We'll take a close look at these passages later on.

Other Elements

SETTING

The setting in *The Great Gatsby* is very important because in Fitzgerald's world *setting* reveals *character*. Fitzgerald divides the world of the novel into four major settings: 1. East Egg; 2. West Egg; 3. the valley of ashes; and 4. New York City. Within these major settings are two or more subsettings. East Egg is limited to Daisy's house, but West Egg incorporates both Gatsby's house and Nick's. The valley of ashes includes the Wilson's garage, Michaelis' restaurant, and the famous sign with the eyes of Dr. T. J. Eckleburg. New York City includes the offices where people work, the apartment Tom Buchanan has rented for Myrtle Wilson, and the Plaza Hotel, where the final showdown between Gatsby and Tom Buchanan takes place.

Each of these settings both reflects and determines the values of the people who live or work there. East Egg, where Tom and Daisy live, is the home of the Ivy League set who have had wealth for a long time and are comfortable with it. Since they are secure with their money, they have no need to show it off. Nick lives in new-rich West Egg because he is too poor to afford a home in East Egg; Gatsby lives there because his money is "new" and he lacks the social credentials to be accepted in East Egg. His house, like the rest of his possessions (his pink suit, for example), is tasteless and vulgar and would be completely out of place in the more refined and understated world of East Egg. No wonder that Gatsby is ruined in the end by the East, and that Nick decides to leave.

The valley of ashes in contrast to both Eggs is where the poor people live—those who are the victims of the rich. It is characterized literally by dust, for it is here that the city's ashes are dumped (in what is now Flushing, Queens), and the inhabitants are, as it were, symbolically dumped on by the rest of the world. The valley of ashes, with its brooding eyes of Dr. T. J. Eckleburg, also stands as a symbol of the spiritual dryness, the emptiness of the world of the novel.

New York City is a symbol of what America has become in the 1920s: a place where anything goes, where money is made and bootleggers flourish, and where the World Series can be fixed by a man like Meyer Wolfsheim. New York is a place of parties and affairs, and bizarre and colorful characters who appear from time to time in West Egg at Gatsby's parties.

The idea of setting as moral geography is reinforced by the overriding symbolism of the American East and the American Midwest. This larger contrast between East and Midwest frames the novel as a whole. Nick comes East to enter the bond business, and finds himself instead in the dizzying world of The Jazz Age in the summer of 1922. He is fascinated and disgusted with this world, and he eventually returns home to the Midwest, to the values and traditions of his youth.

THEMES

A good novel has a number of themes. The following are important themes of *The Great Gatsby*.

1. THE CORRUPTION OF THE AMERICAN DREAM

The American Dream—as it arose in the Colonial period and developed in the nineteenth century—was based on the assumption that each person, no matter what his origins, could succeed in life on the sole basis of his or her own skill and effort. The dream was embodied in the ideal of the self-made man, just as it was embodied in Fitzgerald's own family by his grandfather, P. F. McQuillan.

The Great Gatsby is a novel about what happened to the American dream in the 1920s, a period when the old values that gave substance to the dream had been corrupted by the vulgar pursuit of wealth. The characters are Midwesterners who have come East in pursuit of this new dream of money, fame, success, glamour, and excitement. Tom and Daisy must have a huge house, a stable of polo ponies, and friends in Europe. Gatsby must have his enormous mansion before he can feel confident enough to try to win Daisy.

What Fitzgerald seems to be criticizing in *The Great Gatsby* is not the American Dream itself but the corruption of the American Dream. What was once—for Ben Franklin, for example, or Thomas Jefferson—a belief in self-reliance and hard work has become what Nick Carraway calls ". . . the service of a vast, vulgar, and meretricious beauty." The energy that might have gone into the pursuit of noble goals has been channeled into the pursuit of power and pleasure, and a very showy, but fundamentally empty form of success.

How is this developed? I have tried to indicate in the chapter-by-chaper analysis, especially in the Notes, that Fitzgerald's critique of the dream of success is developed primarily through the five central characters and through certain dominant images and symbols. The characters might be divided into three groups: 1. Nick, the observer and commentator, who sees what has gone wrong; 2. Gatsby, who lives the dream purely; and 3. Tom, Daisy, and Jordan, the "foul dust" who are the prime examples of the corruption of the dream.

The primary images and symbols that Fitzgerald employs in developing the theme are: 1. the green light; 2. the eyes of Dr. T.J. Eckleburg; 3. the imagery of the East and Midwest; 4. Owl Eyes; 5. Dan Cody's yacht; and 6. religious terms such as *grail* and *incarnation*.

2. SIGHT AND INSIGHT

Both the character groupings and the images and symbols suggest a second major theme that we can call "sight and insight." As you read the novel, you will come across many images of blindness; is this because hardly anyone seems to see what is really going on? The characters have little self-knowledge and even less knowledge of each other. Even Gatsby—we might say, especially Gatsby—lacks the insight to understand what is happening. He never truly *sees* either Daisy or himself, so blinded is he by his dream. The only characters who see, in the sense of "understand," are Nick and Owl Eyes. The ever present eyes of Dr. Eckleburg seem to reinforce the theme that there is no all-seeing presence in the modern world.

3. THE MEANING OF THE PAST

The past is of central importance in the novel, whether it is Gatsby's personal past (his affair with Daisy in 1917) or the larger historical past to which Nick refers in the closing sentence of the novel: "So we beat on, boats against the current, borne back ceaselessly into the past." The past holds something that both Gatsby and Nick seem to long for: a simpler, better, nobler time, perhaps, a time when people believed in the importance of the family and the church. Tom, Daisy and Jordan are creatures of the present—Fitzgerald tells us little or nothing about their pasts—and it is this allegiance to the moment that makes them so attractive, and also so rootless and spiritually empty.

4. THE EDUCATION OF A YOUNG MAN

In Chapter VII, Nick remembers that it is his thirtieth birthday. He, like Gatsby, Tom, and Daisy, came East to get away from his past; now that his youth is officially over, he realizes that he may have made a mistake to come East, and begins a period of reevaluation that leads to his eventual decision to return to the Middle West.

The Great Gatsby is the story of Nick's initiation into life. His trip East gives him the education he needs to grow up. The novel can, therefore, be called a *bildungsroman*—the German word for a story about a young man. (Other examples of a *bildungsroman* are *The Red Badge of Courage, David Copperfield*, and *The Catcher in the Rye*.) Nick, in a sense, writes *The Great Gatsby* to show us what he has learned.

STYLE

Style refers to the way a writer puts words together: the length and rhythm of his sentences; his use of figurative language and symbolism; his use of dialogue and description.

Fitzgerald called *The Great Gatsby* a "novel of selected incident," modelled after Flaubert's *Madame Bovary*. "What I cut out of it both physically and emotionally would make another novel," he said. Fitzgerald's stylistic method is to let a part stand for the whole. In Chapters I to III, for example, he lets three parties stand for the whole summer and for the contrasting values of three different worlds. He also lets small snatches of dialogue represent what is happening at each party. The technique is cinematic. The "camera" zooms in, gives us a snatch of conversation, and then cuts to another group of people. Nick serves almost as a recording device, jotting down what he hears. Fitzgerald's ear for dialogue, especially for the colloquial phrases of the period, is excellent.

Fitzgerald's style might also be called *imagistic*. His language is full of images—concrete verbal pictures appealing to the senses. There is water imagery in descriptions of the rain, Long Island Sound, and the swimming pool. There is religious imagery in the Godlike eyes of Dr. Eckleburg and in words such as *incarnation*, and *grail*. There is color imagery: pink for Gatsby, yellow and white for Daisy.

Some images might more properly be called symbols for the way they point beyond themselves to historic or mythic truths: the green light at the end of Daisy's dock, for instance, or Dr. Eckleburg's eyes, or Dan Cody's yacht. Through the symbolic use of images, Fitzgerald transforms what is on the surface a realistic social novel of the 1920s into a myth about America.

Finally, we might call Fitzgerald's style reflective. There are several important passages at which Nick stops and reflects on the meaning of the action, almost interpreting the events. The style in such passages is dense, intellectual, almost deliberately difficult as Nick tries to wrestle with the meanings behind the events he has witnessed.

POINT OF VIEW

Style and point of view are very hard to separate in a novel that is told in the first person by a narrator who is also one of the characters. The voice is always

Nick's. Fitzgerald's choice of Nick as the character through whom to tell his story has a stroke of genius. He had been reading Joseph Conrad and had been particularly struck by the way in which Conrad uses the character of Marlow to tell both the story of Kurtz in *Heart of Darkness* and the story of Jim in *Lord Jim*. In those novels, Fitzgerald learned, we never see the characters of Kurtz or Jim directly, but only through the eyes of other people. And when we come to think of it, isn't that how we get to know people in real life? We never get to know them all at once, as we get to know characters described by an omniscient novelist; we learn about them in bits and pieces over a period of time. And so, Fitzgerald reasoned, someone like Gatsby would be much more understandable and sympathetic if presented through the eyes of a character like ourselves. Rather than imposing himself between us and the action, Nick brings us closer to the action by forcing us to experience events as though we were Nick. The *I* of the novel becomes ourselves, and we find ourselves, like Nick, wondering who Gatsby is, why he gives these huge parties, and what his past and background may be. By writing from Nick's point of view, Fitzgerald is able to make Gatsby more realistic than he could have by presenting Gatsby through the eyes of an omniscient narrator. He is also able to make Gatsby a more sympathetic character because of Nick's decision to become Gatsby's friend. We want to find out more about Gatsby because Nick does. We care about Gatsby because Nick does. We are angry that no one comes to Gatsby's funeral because Nick is.

The use of the limited first person point of view gives not only the character of Gatsby but the whole novel a greater air of realism. We believe these parties really happened because a real person named Nick

Carraway is reporting what he saw. When Nick writes down the names of the people who came to Gatsby's parties on a Long Island Railroad timetable, we believe that these people actually came to Gatsby's parties.

Nick is careful throughout the novel never to tell us things that he could not have known. If he was not present at a particular occasion, he gets the information from someone who was—from Jordan Baker, for example, who tells him about Gatsby's courtship of Daisy in Louisville; or from the Greek, Michaelis, who tells him about the death of Myrtle Wilson. Sometimes Nick summarizes what others tell him, and sometimes he uses their words. But he never tells us something he could never know. This is one of the reasons the novel is so convincing.

FORM AND STRUCTURE

Form and structure are closely related to point of view. Before writing a novel, an author has to ask himself: who is to tell the story? And in what order will events be told? The primary problem in answering the second question is how to handle time. Do I tell the story straight through from beginning to end? Do I start in the middle and use flashbacks?

As many critics have pointed out, the method Fitzgerald adopts in *The Great Gatsby* is a brilliant one. He starts the novel in the present, giving us, in the first three chapters, a glimpse of the four main locales of the novel: Daisy's house in East Egg (Chapter I); the valley of ashes and New York (Chapter II); and Gatsby's house in West Egg (Chapter III). Having established the characters and setting in the first three chapters, he then narrates the main events of the story in Chapters IV to IX, using Chapters IV, VI, and VIII to gradually reveal the story of Gatsby's past. The past and present come together at the end of the novel in Chapter IX.

The critic James E. Miller, Jr., diagrams the sequence of events in *The Great Gatsby* like this: "Allowing *X* to stand for the straight chronological account of the summer of 1922, and *A, B, C, D,* and *E* to represent the significant events of Gatsby's past, the nine chapters of *The Great Gatsby* may be charted: *X, X, X, XCX, X, XBXCX, X, XCXDXD, XEXAX.*"

Miller's diagram shows clearly how Fitzgerald designed the novel. He gives us the information as Nick gets it, just as we might find out information about a friend or acquaintance in real life, in bits and pieces over a period of time. Since we don't want or can't absorb much information about a character until we truly become interested in him, Fitzgerald waits to take us into the past until close to the middle of the novel. As the story moves toward its climax, we find out more and more about the central figure from Nick until we, too, are in a privileged position and can understand *why* Gatsby behaves as he does.

Thus the key to the structure of the novel is the combination of the first person narrative and the gradual revelation of the past as the narrator finds out more and more. The two devices work extremely effectively together, but neither would work very well alone.

Note that the material included in the novel is highly selective. Fitzgerald creates a series of scenes—most of them parties—but does not tell us much about what happens between these scenes. Think of how much happened in the summer of 1922 that Fitzgerald *doesn't* tell us! He doesn't tell us about Gatsby and Daisy's relationship after they meet at Nick's house in Chapter V, because Nick would have no access to this information. What the technique of extreme selectivity demands from the reader is close attention. We have to piece together everything we know about Gatsby from the few details that Nick gives us. Part of the pleasure this form gives us is that of drawing conclusions not only from what is included but from what is left out.

The Story

CHAPTER I

The opening paragraphs teach us a lot about Nick and his attitude toward Gatsby and others. Nick introduces himself to us as a young man from the Midwest who has come East to learn the bond business. He tells us that he's tolerant, inclined to reserve judgment about people, and a good listener. People tell him their secrets because they trust him; he knows the story of Gatsby.

If you read closely, you'll see that Nick has ambivalent feelings toward Gatsby. He both loves Gatsby and is critical of him. Nick is tolerant, but that toleration has limits. He hates Gatsby's crass and vulgar materialism, but he also admires the man for his dream, his "romantic readiness," his "extraordinary gift for hope."

Nick makes the distinction between Gatsby, whom he loves because of his dream, and the other characters, who constitute the "foul dust" that "floated in the wake of his dreams." Nick has such scorn for these "Eastern" types that he has left the East, returned to the Midwest, and, for the time being at least, withdraws from his involvement with other people.

Having told us about his relationships, Nick now introduces us to the world in which he lived during the summer of 1922: the world of East Egg and West Egg, Long Island.

Fitzgerald designed *The Great Gatsby* very carefully, establishing each of the locations in the novel as a symbol for a particular style of life. West Egg, where Nick and Gatsby live, is essentially a place for the *nouveau riche*. There are two types of people living here:

those on the way up the social ladder who have not the family background or the money to live in fashionable East Egg; and those like Gatsby, whose vulgar display of wealth and connections with Broadway or the New York underworld make them unwelcome in the more dignified world of East Egg. Nick describes his own house as an eyesore, but it is a smaller eyesore than Gatsby's mansion, which has a tower on one side, "spanking new under a thin beard of raw ivy." Words like *new, thin,* and *raw* describe some of the reasons Gatsby's house is a monstrosity.

By contrast, East Egg is like a fairyland. Its primary color is white, and Nick calls its houses "white palaces" that glitter in the sunlight. The story actually opens in East Egg on the night Nick drives over to have dinner with Tom and Daisy Buchanan. Since Daisy is his cousin and Tom, a friend from Yale, Nick has the credentials to visit East Egg. Their house is "a cheerful red-and-white Georgian Colonial Mansion" overlooking the bay. And the owner is obviously proud of his possessions.

Our first view of Tom Buchanan reveals a very powerful man standing in riding clothes with his legs apart on his front porch. He likes his power, and like the potentates of Eastern kingdoms, he expects the obedience of his subjects. We are ushered into the living room with its "frosted wedding cake" ceiling, its wine-colored rug, and its enormous couch on which are seated two princesses in white: Jordan Baker and Tom's wife, Daisy Buchanan. Fitzgerald controls the whole scene through his use of colors—white and gold mainly—that suggest a combination of beauty and wealth. Yet underneath this magical surface there is something wrong. Jordan Baker is bored and discontented. She yawns more than once in this very first scene. There is something cool and slightly unpleasant about the atmosphere—something basically disturbing. Tom talks about a book he has read, *The Rise of the Colored Empires* by Goddard. It is a piece of pure Social Darwinism, advocating that the white race preserve its own purity and beat down the colored races before they rise up and overcome the whites. Daisy, who seems not to understand what Tom is talking about, teases him about his size and about the big words in the book. The telephone rings, and Tom is called from the room to answer it. When Daisy follows him out, Jordan Baker confides to Nick that the call is from Tom's woman in New York.

The rest of the evening is awkward and painful as Tom and Daisy try unsuccessfully to forget the intrusion. Daisy's cynicism about life becomes painfully clear when she says about her daughter's birth: " 'I'm glad it's a girl. And I hope she'll be a fool—that's the best thing a girl can be in this world, a beautiful little fool.' "

NOTE: Under the veneer of the white world, there is hollowness. Nick has said at the very beginning that "Gatsby turned out all right at the end; it is what preyed on Gatsby, what foul dust floated in the wake of his dreams that temporarily closed out my interest in the abortive sorrows and short-winded elations of men." Even in this opening chapter, we are getting hints that Tom and Daisy are part of this foul dust.

In Nick's eyes, Tom and Daisy belong to "a rather distinguished secret society," whose members have powers the outside world can neither understand nor control. Nick finds both of them smug and insincere.

The evening ends early, around ten o'clock. Jordan Baker, a competitive golfer, wants to go to bed since she's playing in a tournament the next day. Before Nick leaves for West Egg, Tom and Daisy hint that they would welcome his attention to Miss Baker during the summer.

Nick arrives home, and (in the final paragraph of the chapter) gets his first glimpse of Gatsby. Gatsby is standing on the lawn, stretching out "his arms toward the dark water in a curious way." Nick, from his own house, believes that he can see Gatsby trembling. As Nick looks out at the water, he can see ". . . nothing except a single green light, minute and far away, that might have been the end of a dock."

NOTE: The Green Light As Symbol This is the first use of one of the novel's central symbols, the green light at the end of Daisy's dock. What Fitzgerald seems to be doing is merely introducing a symbol that will gain in meaning as the story progresses. At this point, we don't even know that the light is on Daisy's dock, and we have no reason to associate Gatsby with Daisy. What we do know—and this is very important—is that Nick admires Gatsby because of his dream and this dream is somehow associated with the green light. The color green is a traditional symbol of spring and hope and youth. As long as Gatsby gazes at the green light, his dream lives.

The might meet Daisy

CHAPTER II

The opening description of the valley of ashes, watched over by the brooding eyes of Dr. T.J. Eckleburg, has been analyzed again and again. Fitzgerald's friend and editor, Maxwell Perkins, wrote to Scott on

November 20, 1924: "In the eyes of Dr. Eckleburg various readers will see different significances; but their presence gives a superb touch to the whole thing: great unblinking eyes, expressionless, looking down upon the human scene. It's magnificent." Later in the same letter Perkins concludes, ". . . with the help of T.J. Eckleburg . . . you have imported a sort of sense of eternity."

How should you approach this famous symbol? Remember, a wide variety of interpretations have been made and defended over the years.

It's best to begin by placing Eckleburg in his geographical context: the valley of ashes, located about halfway between West Egg and New York City. The valley of ashes is the home of George and Myrtle Wilson, whom we'll meet later on in this chapter. The valley is also a very important part of what we might call the *moral geography* of the novel. Values are associated with places. In Chapter I we were introduced to East and West Egg, the homes of the very rich, the *nouveau riche*, and the middle class. The valley of ashes is the home of the poor, the victims of those who live in either New York or the Eggs. Men, described by Fitzgerald as "ash-gray," move through the landscape "dimly and already crumbling through the powdery air."

Apparently the city's ashes are dumped in the valley, and the men who work here have the job of shovelling up these ashes with "leaden spades."

NOTE: On a more symbolic level, these men are inhabitants of what might be called Fitzgerald's wasteland. T.S. Eliot's famous poem "The Waste Land" had been published in 1922, and Fitzgerald had read it with great interest. There is no doubt that he had Eliot's poem in mind when he described the valley of ashes. Eliot's wasteland—arid, desertlike—contains figures who go through the motions of life with no spiritual center. Eliot's imagery seemed to express the anxiety, frustration, and emptiness of a post-war generation cut off from spiritual values by the shock of the First World War.

Read the following passage carefully:

> The eyes of Doctor T.J. Eckleburg are blue and gigantic—their retinas are one yard high. They look out of no face, but, instead, from a pair of enormous yellow spectacles which pass over a non-existent nose. Evidently some wild wag of an oculist set them there to fatten his practice in the borough of Queens, and then sank down himself into eternal blindness, or forgot them and moved away. But his eyes, dimmed a little by many paintless days under sun and rain, brood on over the solemn dumping ground.

Some readers interpret this passage as a description of the god of the modern world—the god of the wasteland. Keep this description in mind in Chapter VIII when the crazed and jealous Wilson looks at the giant eyes and says, "God sees everything." For now, early in Chapter II, it is still too early to make any kind of direct correlation between the eyes of Dr. Eckleburg and the eyes of God. At this point we have only hints: the size of the eyes, the missing face, the departure of the original creator of the sign, all of which transform the eyes into something mythic, something suggesting a superior being who no longer cares, who is no longer involved with the petty lives of the pathetic creatures below. The eyes "brood on over the solemn dumping ground," offering no help or solace to its inhabitants. The oculist has forgotten the eyes which he left behind, just as God has forgotten the inhabitants of the valley of ashes. Many interpretations are possible; you'll want to think about them as the novel develops.

The action of the second chapter begins as Tom Buchanan brings Nick to George B. Wilson's garage. Both the garage and the all-night restaurant of the Greek Michaelis border the valley of ashes. Wilson's wife, Myrtle, is Tom's mistress. Pay close attention to these first descriptions of Wilson and his wife, and you'll learn a lot about who they are and what they stand for. Wilson is described as "a blond, spiritless man, anaemic, and faintly handsome." He is the embodiment of the valley of ashes: dead inside, a living ghost. The key words are *spiritless* and *anaemic*. He has no energy and no faith. He believes somehow that doing business with Tom will help him; but he understands neither the power nor the cruelty of the man he is dealing with. Myrtle Wilson is a sensuous woman in her middle thirties who has the energy her husband lacks. "There was an immediate perceptible vitality about her," says Nick. The fire inside her has drawn her to Tom Buchanan as a lover who can take her away from the gray and empty prison of the valley of ashes.

Note that Tom takes Myrtle to New York, the fourth major location in the moral geography of the novel. If the valley of ashes is the home of death-in-life—the place where the spiritless and downtrodden live—New York is the center of the corruption, or, more appropriately, the place where wealth, corruption, and self-gratification openly meet. Myrtle must ride into New York on the train in a separate car in deference to the "East Eggers." Why? Because it is important to keep up a façade of respectability. In New York, however, where anything is permitted, Tom can flaunt his relationship with Myrtle.

The group goes to the apartment in Morningside Heights that Tom Buchanan has rented for his liaisons with Myrtle. What goes on there and how Nick reacts to what goes on tell us something very important about how Fitzgerald wants us to view New York.

The party consists of Nick, Tom, Myrtle, Myrtle's sister Catherine, and a couple named McKee who live downstairs. Nick is really more of an observer than a participant. He tells us that he has been drunk just twice in his life, and the second time was that afternoon. Whether he drinks in order to lose his self-control and join the others or simply to escape this disordered world is something you'll have to decide for yourself. Perhaps both interpretations are correct. In any case, all the guests at the party seem to have something unnatural or wrong with them. Catherine, the sister, has "a solid, sticky bob of red hair, and a complexion powdered milky white. Her eyebrows had been plucked and then drawn on again at a more rakish angle." Mr. McKee is a pale, feminine man who has just shaved and left a spot of lather on his cheek. His wife is "shrill, languid, handsome and horrible." Myrtle Wilson becomes more and more "violently affected moment by moment." The conversation is absurd and pretentious; everyone tries to impress each other, and lies flow as freely as the liquor.

Nick tries to leave; part of him wants to be somewhere else, but part of him—that part that makes him the narrator of this novel—is fascinated by "the inexhaustible variety of life." He is both repelled and attracted toward these people. The appearance of Myrtle Wilson's new puppy, "groaning faintly," is like the entire scene, both funny and sad. Then a crisis erupts. Myrtle crudely insists that she can say, "Daisy!" any time she wants, and Tom Buchanan, making a short deft movement, breaks her nose with his open hand. So this is what happens to those who become entangled with the Buchanans! Tom, we see, is strong and brutal and absolutely selfish. He is perfectly happy to enjoy Myrtle in bed, but at other times she must know when to keep her place. For challenging the purity of his Daisy, she is punished. Later, in Chapter VII during the second New York party, we'll see what happens when Gatsby tries to cross Tom Buchanan.

In two chapters, Fitzgerald has shown us two different symbolic landscapes: one, a dinner party in East Egg with Daisy, Jordan, Tom and Nick; the other, a drunken brawl in New York with Tom, Nick, Myrtle, Catherine and the McKees. The contrast between the two parties tells us much about these two worlds and about the people who inhabit them. Now to complete his introduction to the world of the novel, Fitzgerald gives us in Chapter III a third party—at the West Egg Home of Jay Gatsby.

CHAPTER III

Though the novel is called *The Great Gatsby*, we have neither seen Gatsby (except for a glimpse of him at the end of Chapter I) nor been given any idea of why he should be called "great." Fitzgerald's method is to introduce Gatsby to us gradually, as a kind of mystery to be solved. We see Gatsby first through the eyes of others. Catherine Wilson told Nick (in Chapter II) that she had heard that Gatsby was a nephew or a cousin of Kaiser Wilhelm's. Lucille, a friend of Jordan Baker, thinks that Gatsby was a German spy during the war. A man sitting nearby agrees with her. The world is full of rumors about Gatsby because no one really knows who he is, where his money comes from, and why he gives these magnificent parties every weekend. Our job as readers is to separate fact from rumor and to discover, with Nick, who Gatsby really is and why he behaves the way he does. Our job will be to probe behind the vulgar, violent surface of his world to reveal the man beneath. We are able to do that—as in real life—only gradually, for it is never possible to know someone all at once. The process begins in Chapter III with a portrait of the public Gatsby, seen through the eyes of his guests. It's not until Chapter IV that we'll begin to discover the man beneath.

Brightness, confusion, magnificence, daring, vulgarity, excess, excitement—these are the words that describe Gatsby's parties. They also describe one side of life in America during the 1920s, in the years before the Great Depression. Gatsby has a Rolls Royce, a station wagon, two motor boats, aquaplanes, a swimming pool, and a real beach. People come to his parties and *use* these things. Everything is *real.* Crates of oranges and lemons are delivered to his door. Beneath canvas tents in the garden are buffet tables glittering with spiced hams and turkeys "bewitched to a dark gold." Gatsby's bar is stocked with gin, liquors, and "cordials so long forgotten that most of his female guests were too young to know one from another." The world of Gatsby's parties has an aura of magic about it—not the magic of East Egg, with its fairytale imagery of princesses in ivory towers, but the magic of the amusement park, with the promise of fast rides and expensive prizes. Gatsby's world is a world of infinite hope and possibility. Young girls with laughter like gold wait for the right man. Middle-aged women, tired of their husbands, search for lovers. And ambitious men search for the right contact that will bring them instant fame and fortune.

Nobody knows the host. Nick is "one of the few guests who had actually been invited." Fitzgerald builds suspense by making us wonder when we'll meet Gatsby and what he'll be like when we do. Nick runs into Jordan Baker and the twins, who talk about Gatsby, but have only false information about him. Nick and Jordan go off in search of Gatsby, but discover Owl Eyes instead.

NOTE: Owl Eyes Owl Eyes is "a stout middle-aged man, with enormous owl-eyed spectacles." He is overwhelmed by the fact that Gatsby's Gothic library is stocked not with the fake, cardboard backs of books, but with the works themselves. He knows that Gatsby has never read the books, however, because the pages have never been cut. " 'This fella's a regular Belasco,' " Owl Eyes tells Nick and Jordan. " 'It's a triumph. . . . Knew when to stop, too—didn't cut the pages.' "

The reference to David Belasco, the great playwright-producer-director of realistic plays, is not accidental. Owl Eyes, as Nick refers to him, is the first to realize the essentially theatrical quality of Gatsby's world. Just as Belasco was a technician who wanted to get everything right, so Gatsby spares no expense to build the material world necessary to fulfill his dream. He has created an extraordinary stage set complete with real books. Owl Eyes, as his name suggests, is one of the few to really *see* and, in some way, understand Gatsby.

Nick and Jordan go back outside to watch the entertainment at midnight. Even the moon cooperates, floating over Long Island sound like the cardboard moon on a stage set. In a scene that Nick calls "significant, elemental, profound," Gatsby appears:

> "I'm Gatsby," he said suddenly.
>
> "What!" I exclaimed. "Oh, I beg your pardon."
>
> "I thought you knew, old sport. I'm afraid I'm not a very good host."
>
> He smiled understandingly—much more than understandingly. It was one of those rare smiles with a quality of eternal reassurance in it, that you may come across four or five times in life. It faced—or seemed to face—the whole external world for an instant, and then concentrated on *you* with an irresistible prejudice in your favor. It understood you just as far as you wanted to be understood, believed in you as you would like to believe in yourself, and assured you that it had precisely the impression of you that, at your best, you hoped to convey. Precisely at that point it vanished—and I was looking at an elegant young roughneck, a year or two over thirty, whose elaborate formality of speech just missed being absurd.

Gatsby is a series of paradoxes. He is both a "roughneck" and one who practices "elaborate formality in speech." He calls people "old sport," apparently a habit picked up at Oxford, though at this point we're still uncertain whether Oxford is just part of the myth. Has he really gone to Oxford? We, like Jordan Baker, may not believe it. But then why is he picking his words with care? And how did he earn the money to give these parties? As Nick points out: people don't just "drift cooly out of nowhere and buy a palace on Long Island Sound." A millionaire who gives parties conjures up an image of a "florid and corpulent person in his middle years." But Gatsby is none of these.

Gatsby is—quite simply—not like anyone else in the world of the novel. Young, handsome, excessively polite, he seems not to belong to the world he has created. His smile radiates an inner warmth that his guests don't have. Nick alone senses it. "Anyway, he gives large parties," says Jordan Baker, because the party, not Gatsby, is what interests her. But now Nick watches Gatsby as much as he watches the party. He notices Gatsby standing "alone on the marble steps and looking from one group to another with approving eyes." Here Gatsby is like a director admiring his play or a religious leader blessing his disciples. He alone is not drinking. As the party grows more frenzied, he becomes increasingly separate from it. He is untouched by the corruption of the world.

The party goes on. People become more drunk and irritable. Husbands and wives fight over whether to stay or leave. Some wives are lifted, kicking into their cars. Gatsby goes to answer a telephone call from Philadelphia at 2 A.M. As Nick leaves to walk home, he encounters Owl Eyes, who is unable to get his car out of the ditch. Neither Owl Eyes nor the car's driver—"a pale, dangling individual"—seems to be able to manage. Nick returns to his own home, leaving the guests to struggle with their problem.

Nick shifts the focus of the chapter from Gatsby back to himself. He wants us to know that he's done more with his summer than go to parties. To correct that false impression, he tells us how he usually occupies his time. As he tells us about his work, his walks through New York City, and his fascination for women, he gives us a sense that, in some way he is as hollow as the characters he describes. He seems to need adventure as an escape from loneliness, and perhaps that is what draws him to Jordan Baker. He is also sexually attracted to her. He became involved with Jordan around midsummer, he tells us, after a short affair with a girl from Jersey City. He knows that Jordan is dishonest—she cheated in her first golf tournament by moving her ball to improve her lie. Whatever Nick's reason for being with her, we're made to feel that somehow Jordan is not the kind of woman Nick *ought* to like.

At the end of the chapter Nick says, "Every one suspects himself of at least one of the cardinal virtues, and this is mine; I am one of the few honest people that I have ever known." This is one of the most talked about lines in the novel, and it is a hard one to interpret, coming as it does right after Nick's statement that "dishonesty in a woman is a thing you never blame deeply." Is Nick using a double standard, arguing that it's all right for women to be dishonest because they can't help it? How do we reconcile our view of Nick as a reliable and sympathetic narrator when he allows himself to get involved with such a morally unattractive woman? These are questions raised by the troubling last pages of this chapter—questions that are answered in a variety of ways by different readers. If you want to question Nick's judgment, you can certainly find evidence to support that point of view. Yet most readers have not been too hard on Nick for his relationship with Jordan. The question is very much an open one.

CHAPTER IV

One of the extraordinary things about *The Great Gatsby* is that the action of the novel (call it the plot, if you want) doesn't start until Chapter IV. We have had three parties, and we have been introduced to all the major characters. Finally, we are allowed to find out why they have been brought together and what the nature of the *story* is in which they all share. But before Fitzgerald begins that story, he has one more set of details to give us: a list of the people who came to Gatsby's parties during the summer of 1922.

NOTE: The Guests at Gatsby's Parties Why does Fitzgerald give us a list of guests nearly three pages long? Perhaps he wants to lend an air of reality to the parties by listing the guests as they would appear in a newspaper report. The names seem to come from social registers, movie magazines, businessmen's directories, and club rosters. Names, as you know, can reveal many things about a person, such as his religion, his ethnic background, and his social class. Judging by Fitzgerald's list, just about every type of person is represented at Gatsby's parties. Names like Flink, Hammerhead, Beluga, Muldoon, Gulick, Fishguard, and Snell suggest humorously that many of these people have no backgrounds at all but belong to a vast vulgar crowd of self-made men, all hungering for success. Fitzgerald's long list of names also makes fun of a technique used in epics such as *The Iliad* and *The Odyssey*. In these heroic poems, we are given lists of warriors. In *The Great Gatsby* we are given lists of guests at parties. Our world of knights and ladies has become much smaller and *much* less noble.

The story continues with Gatsby driving Nick to New York for lunch. Gatsby has decided to use this trip to tell Nick something about himself. Our first reaction, like Nick's, is one of disbelief. Gatsby's words are so full of lies that it's difficult to know whether anything he says is true. He tells Nick that he's the son of wealthy people in the Midwest, "all dead now." He claims to have been educated at Oxford. When Nick asks him where in the Midwest he's from, Gatsby answers, "San Francisco." The lie is so blatant that we don't know what to make of it. Neither does Nick. Gatsby continues to describe his life as that of a "young rajah in all the capitals of Europe," collecting jewels, hunting for big game. Then he speaks of his war experience, his heroism, and the medals he was awarded by various European governments, "even Montenegro." At this point, when Nick is most incredulous, Gatsby produces from his pocket his medal from Montenegro and a picture of himself with cricket bat standing in the quad at one of the colleges at Oxford. There is thus a bizarre mixture of truth and fantasy in Gatsby's self-description, and we are forced both to hold him in awe and to reserve final judgment on him until we can find out more. The car carrying Nick and Gatsby to New York seems to fly—gliding through the valley of ashes, soaring through Astoria. A policeman stops them for speeding, but apologizes to Gatsby as soon as Gatsby shows him a white card. As the car enters New York, Nick is struck anew by the appropriateness of that city as a place for Gatsby to do business. The suspense over Gatsby's true identity and purpose is sustained throughout the chapter, first at lunch, and then in the tea scene with Jordan Baker.

NOTE: Meyer Wolfsheim At lunch we are introduced to the business side of Gatsby in the person of Meyer Wolfsheim. Wolfsheim is modeled on the real-life figure of Arnold Rothstein, the man who helped fix the 1919 World Series. Through Wolfsheim, "a small flat-nosed Jew," we learn about Gatsby's connections with a shady underworld, and we begin to understand for the first time where Gatsby's money comes from. The discovery of Gatsby's unsavory business dealings may taint his dreams for you and make you question his "greatness." But you may also find that it lends him an air of mystery and romance.

Wolfsheim is sentimental about friends but not about business—something we will learn again at the end of the novel. He mistakes Nick for one of Gatsby's business friends and asks him if he's looking for a "gonnegtion." But when he finds out that Nick is merely a personal friend, he changes the subject. Wolfsheim has neither education nor class. When Gatsby leaves the room for a phone call (Gatsby is always leaving rooms for important and mysterious phone calls), Wolfsheim tells Nick that Gatsby has gone to "Oggsford College in England." Oxford, as a point of fact, is a university; there is no Oxford College. Wolfsheim is so uncultured that he's impressed with Gatsby's breeding and considers Gatsby "the kind of man you'd like to take home and introduce to your mother and sister." He's so bad at judging other people that he describes Gatsby as someone who would never so much as look at another man's wife. Nothing says more about Wolfsheim's boorishness and his ruthless battle for money and power than the fact that he wears cuff links made of human molars. The scene is full of wonderful ironic touches such as this, which Nick simply relates without commenting on.

From Jordan Baker, Nick learns about Gatsby and Daisy. She begins as though she were telling a fairy-tale. And indeed it is. The princess in this case is Daisy Fay, an eighteen-year-old beauty, the most popular girl in Louisville, Kentucky. All the officers from nearby Camp Taylor are competing for the honor of her company. On this particular day, she is sitting in her white dress in her white roadster (princesses must wear white) with a young lieutenant who is speaking to her with the kind of romantic intensity that princesses adore. His name is Jay Gatsby. Daisy apparently loves him as much as he loves her, for she's ready to go to New York to say good-bye to him when he's sent overseas. And even though she decides to marry Tom Buchanan, she drinks herself into a state of near stupor on the night before her wedding after having received a letter from Gatsby.

Jordan goes on to describe the three years of marriage: Daisy's devotion to Tom and Tom's affairs with a chambermaid in a Santa Barbara hotel. Since we already know that Tom is having an affair with Myrtle Wilson, it doesn't surprise us that Tom has been unfaithful before. What may surprise us is that Daisy seems to have been faithful. Is it because of Gatsby? Does she still love him? Has she thought about him during the five years between their time together in Louisville and the day that she hears his name on Jordan Baker's lips? As Jordan Baker describes it, Daisy has not given Gatsby a thought until the mention of his name jarred her memory. It's hard to say.

In the case of Gatsby, it's not hard to say at all. As Jordan explains, " 'Gatsby bought that house so that Daisy would be just across the bay.' " And Nick responds in a moment of powerful illumination: "Then it had not been merely the stars to which he had aspired on that June night. He came alive to me, delivered suddenly from the womb of his purposeless splendor."

What Nick realizes suddenly is that Gatsby's house and his lavish life-style are not an ostentatious display of wealth, but a necessary means to the fulfillment of his dream. Until now Gatsby was a mystery, misunderstood by many, used by others, reviled as a criminal by still others. Now the truth is unveiled, and we can understand his desperate yearning for Daisy, and for everything—youth, love, and so on—that is symbolized by the green light at the end of Daisy's dock.

Jordan tells Nick that Gatsby had taken her aside at one of his parties and had asked her to ask Nick to ask Daisy to Nick's house for a meeting. This indirection was deliberate, for Gatsby was terrified of seeing Daisy again.

Though Gatsby loves Daisy with an almost unbearable intensity, he doesn't want to offend her or Tom. He's afraid to ask Nick directly, so he uses Jordan as a go-between. Afraid, also, that Daisy will refuse to come to see him, Gatsby arranges for Nick to invite Daisy for tea and makes sure Daisy doesn't know he'll be there, too. Gatsby's elaborate plans show us just how long he has thought about this moment. His plans also reveal the heart of an innocent romantic, a novice at love, who is obviously unused to dealing with women or with situations such as this. We are ready for the central chapter, where the actual meeting takes place.

CHAPTER V

Nick arrives in West Egg to find all the lights in Gatsby's house blazing and Gatsby himself walking toward him across the lawn. Gatsby invites Nick to go to Coney Island. When Nick turns him down, Gatsby suggests a swim in the pool, which he hasn't used all summer. He never does use the pool until the very last day of his life—but that's getting ahead of ourselves.

Nick agrees to invite Daisy over. Gatsby suggests waiting a few days so that he can get Nick's grass cut. Then he offers Nick some money, not a free handout, but a "little business on the side." Here Nick's Midwestern sense of morality helps him make a decision, and he turns Gatsby down.

The day arrives, and it is raining. (Rain in novels is not usually accidental. Notice, as you read this chapter, how the rain stops conveniently at just the right moment.) Gatsby is so nervous that he can hardly function. He has not slept. He is as pale as a high school boy on his first date. Life with Daisy in Louisville had been so wonderful five years before; now he is terrified that even should Daisy agree to renew their relationship, it won't be the same.

Daisy arrives looking absolutely beautiful in a three-cornered lavender hat, "with a bright, ecstatic smile." She is dying to know why Nick has invited her over. Nick takes Daisy inside, thinking that Gatsby is waiting for her, but the living room is empty. Gatsby, either unable to face the encounter or anxious to pretend that he has just dropped over, has gone out into the rain and walked around the house. Now he knocks on the front door. Nick opens it and sees Gatsby, "pale as death," standing in a puddle of water. Both his paleness and the rain reinforce our sense of his fear, his terrible insecurity, and his gloom. Gatsby goes into the living room, leaving Nick in the hall with us to imagine what the first moment must have been like. Apparently it was dreadful, because when Nick does come in the room he finds Gatsby in a state of nerves. Gatsby knocks over Nick's clock (some readers see this as a symbol of his attempt to stop time) and then catches it. The scene has an air of desperate comedy about it; it's funny and not funny at the same time. The characters try to get through tea, and they try to make conversation. When Nick excuses himself, Gatsby rushes into the hall after him, whispering, "This is a terrible mistake."

Nick sends Gatsby back and goes off by himself for half an hour. When Nick returns, the rain has stopped, the sun is out, and Daisy and Gatsby are radiantly happy. Fitzgerald's choice of words to describe Gatsby—"glowed," "new well-being," "radiated," "exultation"—suggest that Gatsby has come alive again. He has rediscovered his dream. He walks Daisy and Nick over to his house and shows them his possessions.

NOTE: Daisy and Gatsby's shirts Suddenly in this scene the meaning of the novel's epigraph becomes clear: the four-line poem of Thomas Park d'Invilliers that Fitzgerald quotes on the title page describes exactly what Gatsby has done. He has symbolically worn the gold hat; he has bounced high, accumulating possessions for *this moment*, so that when Daisy sees them she will cry out, like the lover in the poem, "I must have you." And Daisy does. She admires the house, the gardens, the gigantic rooms, the colors of pink and lavender, the sunken baths. The princess is astounded. Gatsby overwhelms her with these tangible signs of his affection and when he takes his shirts, ordered from England, out of his cabinet and throws them on the bed, she bends her head into the shirts and begins to cry. "They're such beautiful shirts," she sobs. "It makes me sad because I've never seen such beautiful shirts before."

It seems silly of course to cry over shirts. But it is not the shirts themselves that overwhelm her but what they symbolize: Gatsby's extraordinary dedication to his dream. Wouldn't you be moved to tears to find yourself the object of so much adoration?

In the next scene Gatsby tells Daisy about how he has watched the green light that burns at the end of her dock. For so long that light has been a symbol of his dream—of something he has wanted more than life itself. Gazing at it that night when Nick first saw him, and throughout the summer, Gatsby must have believed that if only he could have Daisy he would be happy for ever. Now suddenly he has her, the light is just a light again, and Nick wonders if this person could ever be as wonderful or as magical as Gatsby's *idea* of her. No matter what we think of Gatsby or of his dream, we are drawn to him by the sad knowledge that dreams themselves are often—perhaps always—more beautiful than dreams fulfilled.

Nick realizes this, too, when he says: "There must have been moments even that afternoon when Daisy tumbled short of his dreams—not through her own fault, but because of the colossal vitality of his illusion. It had gone beyond her, beyond everything."

Nick leaves the couple as dusk comes and the lights come on in West Egg. Klipspringer, "the boarder," is summoned from his room to play the piano. As he plays "Ain't We Got Fun?"—one of the most popular songs of the day—we sense a strange irony. What the song is describing is terribly different from what Gatsby and Daisy have at that moment. What they have is so much more than fun: it's beautiful, more intense, and finally more painful. There is both a joy and sadness in a love as great as theirs. Klipspringer plays on, unaware of their feelings. Because Nick *is* aware, he is wise to leave them alone.

CHAPTER VI (Rising action)

This chapter is as important for what it doesn't do as for what it does. In a letter to his friend Edmund Wilson, Fitzgerald confessed about *The Great Gatsby:*

"The worst fault in it, I think, is a BIG FAULT: I gave no account (and had no feeling about or knowledge of) the emotional relations between Gatsby and Daisy from the time of their reunion to the catastrophe." Now since the reunion takes place in Chapter V and the catastrophe, in Chapter VII, the logical place for this account is Chapter VI. Why doesn't it occur?

One reason is that the novel is told in the first person by Nick, and he can describe only what he sees or what he is told by others. What happens between Gatsby and Daisy is private; Nick would have no knowledge of it.

Another reason might be that Fitzgerald wants to emphasize not the actual relationship between Gatsby and Daisy, but Gatsby's dream, and therefore he decided to focus on the past rather than the present. That may explain why in Chapter VI Fitzgerald tells the story of Gatsby's life before he met Daisy—not all of it, but enough for us to begin to understand him.

He was born James Gatz, the son of a North Dakota farmer. He had been sent to St. Olaf College, a small Lutheran school in Minnesota, but had left after two weeks, humiliated by the janitor's job he had been given to pay for his room and board. Having worked in the summer as a clam digger and salmon fisher on Lake Superior, he returned to find a job. It was a decision that changed his life. On Little Girl Bay one day he saw the yacht of copper millionaire Dan Cody in danger of being broken up by a storm, and rowed out to warn him. Cody was impressed by this boy, who called himself Jay Gatsby, and took him on as steward, mate, and later as skipper and personal secretary. In this way, Jay Gatsby was born.

Why did he change his name? In one of the most difficult and important passages in the novel Nick tells us:

> The truth was that Jay Gatsby of West Egg, Long Island, sprang from his Platonic conception of himself. He was a son of God—a phrase which, if it means anything, means just that—and he must be about His Father's business, the service of a vast, vulgar, and meretricious beauty. So he invented just the sort of Jay Gatsby that a seventeen-year-old boy would be likely to invent, and to this conception he was faithful to the end.

NOTE: His Platonic Conception of Himself As a boy Gatsby (still Gatz) had been a dreamer, and as he grew older, his dreams became more vivid. He dreamed, as many children do, of a bright, gaudy world where all his fantasies would be fulfilled. On the day that he saved Dan Cody's yacht, he must have seen an embodiment of everything he wanted. In a strange sort of way Gatsby never believed that he was just James Gatz. He had an *idea* of what he wanted to be. And just as Plato believed that our material bodies are not our real selves, but only physical images of our ideal or perfect selves. Gatsby had an image of himself, to which he gave the name Gatsby. From the day that he met Dan Cody he decided to dedicate his life to the development of the *idea* of himself that existed in his head. And just as Jesus left his family to be about his heavenly Father's business, so Gatsby left his earthly parents to enter the service of his God—a "vast, vulgar, and meretricious beauty"—in this case symbolized by millionaire Dan Cody. Gatsby wanted of course not only to serve Cody but to *be* Dan Cody—one of those remarkable self-made men to come along in America between the 1890s and the years before World War I.

Gatsby sails with Cody to the West Indies and the Barbary Coast. He learns to avoid alcohol when he sees what it does to the older man, and he learns how wonderful the "good life" can be. He decides to devote himself to the pursuit of this life, but Cody dies and his mistress Ella Kaye uses some legal device to steal Gatsby's share of the inheritance. Young Gatsby is once again left penniless. But he has had his "education," and he knows what he wants to be.

At this point Nick's narrative of Gatsby's youth breaks off (notice how we get the story of Gatsby's past in bits and pieces), and we return to the present. It is later in the summer and Nick hasn't seen Gatsby for several weeks. He drops by Gatsby's house and finds Tom Buchanan there. It's the first time these two have been together, and the tension between them, though not as great as it will become, is already strong. Tom has been out riding with a Mr. and Mrs. Sloane. Gatsby invites them to stay for dinner. Mrs. Sloane, who is giving a dinner party herself, invites Nick and Gatsby to join them. Nick politely refuses, but Gatsby accepts—obviously a breach of etiquette, because the invitation was meant as a polite gesture, not as a real offer. Gatsby lacks the social grace to know this; he also wants to be with Daisy. Tom is offended by Gatsby's poor taste. He also doesn't like the idea that Daisy has been coming to Gatsby's house without him. "Women run around too much these days to suit me," he says. "They meet all kinds of crazy fish." Once again we see Tom's double standard (he can do anything he wants) and the snobbery of the East Eggers, who turn their noses up at someone as unrefined as Gatsby.

Even though he disapproves of Gatsby, Tom agrees to visit Gatsby's house the following Saturday night rather than let Daisy go there alone. The rest of Chapter VI describes a second evening at Gatsby's, but this time seen through Daisy's eyes; and the mood is clearly very different from that of the party described in Chapter III.

The people Nick enjoyed only two weeks before now seem "septic" to him. The word *septic* is very strong; it means "putrid" or "rotten." Except for the time she spends alone with Gatsby sitting on Nick's steps, Daisy doesn't have a good time either. The guests seem ill humored, out of control, false. The characters—Doctor Civet, Miss Baedeker, an unnamed movie star and her director, a small producer with a blue nose—all seem part of a phony stage play. Nick compares them to the stars who are here one season, gone the next.

Tom and Daisy argue. Tom is becoming more and more suspicious about who Gatsby is and where he gets his money. Gatsby's nothing more than a big bootlegger, he tells Daisy—which is true. Daisy defends Gatsby with a lie, yet she captures the essence of Gatsby more honestly than Tom's merciless truth.

The chapter ends with a very important scene between Gatsby and Nick after Tom and Daisy have left. Gatsby feels sad because Daisy didn't have a good time, but his sadness goes deeper than that. What really upsets him is that he can't turn back time. "I wouldn't ask too much of her," Nick says. "You can't repeat the past." "Can't repeat the past?" Gatsby cries out in desperation. "Why of course you can!" What Gatsby wants is to obliterate the five years since he last saw Daisy. He wants life to be as wonderful and as beautiful as he believed it could be. Like all of us, he wants to ignore the fact that life is a process of change, and that time never stands still. If only Daisy would tell Tom, "I never loved you!" If only he could take Daisy back to Louisville, marry her, and begin their lives together as though there had been no Tom, no daughter. He must win her to satisfy his own Platonic image of himself, the ideal self which he associates with his love for Daisy in Louisville in the autumn of 1917.

NOTE: Incarnation Fitzgerald uses the word *incarnation* to make us understand the meaning of that moment in Louisville. *Incarnation* means made into flesh, as in the Christian notion that God became flesh in Jesus Christ. In Louisville on the autumn night, Gatsby's dream became incarnated in Daisy. Kissing her for the first time so overpowered him that he knew he must give up everything for her. Gatsby at that moment "wed his unutterable visions to her perishable breath." Because he was only human, he had narrowed his dream and embodied it in something human, something tangible.

The tragedy of Jay Gatsby is his choice of Daisy as the person in whom to embody his dream. This tragedy, as we saw in "The Author and His Times," was not unlike Fitzgerald's own when he embodied his dream in Zelda. Because of the impossibility of their dreams and the nature of the women in whom they vested them, both Gatsby and Scott Fitzgerald were doomed to tragic failure. But that may be why we love them—whether we should or not.

CHAPTER VII

Chapter VII joins all the major characters and geographical locations of the novel together in a final catastrophe. In terms of the action, it is the most important chapter in the novel.

Now that Gatsby has won Daisy, he has called off his parties, fired his servants, and replaced them with friends of Meyer Wolfsheim. His dealings with Wolfsheim reinforce our fears about what he is doing to make his money. His retreat from a glittering nightlife shows us how far his obsession with Daisy has gone. He has dismissed his servants because Daisy has been coming to his house in the afternoons, and he doesn't want anyone around who will gossip. The only reason he gave parties was in the wild hope that Daisy would come—and now she is his.

NOTE: The Weather Fitzgerald carefully orchestrates the weather throughout the novel. The showdown between Tom and Gatsby, for instance, takes place on the hottest day of the summer. The late August heat is oppressive. There is nothing comforting about nature in this modern wasteland; the sun is more a burden than a nourisher of life.

On the appointed day, Nick arrives for lunch at Tom and Daisy's house. Gatsby is there; so is Jordan Baker. All the major figures are together if this were the final scene in a Shakespearean tragedy. The nurse brings in the Buchanans' daughter. Gatsby is stunned; he had never quite believed the child existed until this moment. Drinks are served, and everyone tries to be well mannered, avoiding the issue at hand. But Daisy and Gatsby cannot conceal their love for one another, and Tom sees it.

Daisy has suggested that they go to New York for the afternoon, and Tom now takes her up on it. Notice that they choose New York for the confrontation to come—the same setting that Fitzgerald used for the drunken party in Chapter II. There are close parallels between the two parties, not only in the way the characters behave at them, but in the fact that they have to pass through the valley of ashes to get there.

Jordan, Tom, and Nick ride together in Gatsby's car and stop at Wilson's garage to buy gas. Daisy and Gatsby drive by in Tom's blue coupe, unnoticed by Myrtle Wilson. What Myrtle does notice from her upstairs window is her lover Tom Buchanan, sitting in the yellow Rolls royce with Jordan. Jordan she takes for Daisy.

The whole scene at Wilson's garage has an eerie, mythic quality, as though it were set in a world of its own. Wilson, described literally as "green," has discovered that his wife has been having an affair, but he doesn't know with whom. Myrtle thinks her husband knows it's Tom and watches, "terrified," from the window. Nick realizes that Wilson and Tom are in identical positions—both having just learned that their wives are unfaithful. Wilson wants to take Myrtle away—out West—and Tom begins to feel his whole world collapsing. Over all this, the eyes of Dr. T.J. Eckleburg "kept their vigil." The eyes seem to mock these characters' feeble attempts to hide from the truth. The eyes alone seem to *see* the corruption and the decadence beneath the gorgeous façade.

The yellow Rolls catches up with the blue coupe, and they decide to engage a suite at the Plaza Hotel. It's four o'clock in the afternoon and the heat is overwhelming. Tom, his ego battered by the day's events, mocks Gatsby for calling people "old sport," insinuating that Gatsby never went to Oxford. Gatsby, in a response that delights Nick, simply tells the truth. He attended Oxford for five months after the war through an opportunity offered to some of the officers. Unwilling to let Gatsby get the upper hand, Tom asks him point blank what his intentions are towards Daisy and starts attacking Gatsby about his parties and his life-style. Gatsby, pushed into a corner, responds, " 'Your wife doesn't love you. She's never loved you. She loves me.' "

The two men go after each other, begging Daisy to support them. Gatsby wants Daisy to say she never loved Tom, never in all the years of their marriage. It is this effort to deny the past—to shape the world according to his dream—that brings about Gatsby's downfall. Tom admits he has been less than an ideal husband, but points out " 'Why—there're things between Daisy and me that you'll never know, things that neither of us can ever forget.' " Daisy has tried up to this point to support Gatsby, but now she finds herself turning to Tom. Now that Gatsby's dream has been pierced, Tom finds it easy to tear it to pieces. He has done some investigating of Gatsby's activities and has evidence about his "drug-store" fronts for bootlegging operations. With each thrust, Gatsby's parries become weaker and weaker, and we can feel Daisy slipping slowly but quietly back into the protective camp of her husband. A romantic dream is worth less to her than the security of a husband, unfaithful though he may be. For Gatsby there is nothing left but "the dead dream," which sustains him like a ghostly spirit that fights on after the body is dead. The party is over. Tom has won. He is confident enough to send Gatsby and Daisy home together in Gatsby's yellow car; Gatsby can do no more harm to him. When they leave, Nick realizes that today is his thirtieth birthday.

NOTE: Nick's Thirtieth Birthday Nick's birthday, like the green light and the eyes of Dr. Eckleburg, is one of those symbols that gives the novel's action a deeper meaning. While we identify emotionally with Gatsby, this is Nick's novel too, and his birthday reminds us that it is a novel about Nick's growing up. He came to New York, naïve and inexperienced, having learned about life through books. The summer's events have taught him about life in a way that no book ever could—just as the years on Dan Cody's yacht educated Gatsby. The final phase of his education is learning about death, and death is just around the corner.

Fitzgerald lets us think about death before we know the victim. The suspense works nicely; for a short time we know neither who is dead nor how the person died. Michaelis, the young Greek who runs the all-night restaurant next door to Wilson's garage, tells the story as he experienced it: Myrtle Wilson, who had been locked indoors for most of the day by her husband, had rushed out into the street shortly after seven, frantically waving her arms, only to be struck by a car coming from New York. The car had paused for a moment and then driven on into the night. We are not told whose car it was, but we can guess. Nick, piecing events together from Michaelis' and newspaper accounts, pictures Myrtle Wilson kneeling in the road, her mouth wide open, her "left breast swinging loose like a flap." He wants to emphasize her extraordinary vitality at the moment of her death and the desperate agony with which she tries to hold on to life.

When Tom arrives with Nick and Jordan, his first thought is that Wilson will remember the yellow car from that afternoon. His second thought is that Gatsby was the driver. Tom has his dreams, small as they may be, and he could never let himself believe that Daisy might have been at the wheel.

As for Nick, he has had enough of all of these Easterners. When he arrives with the others at Tom's house, he remains outside. Suddenly, Gatsby calls to him from the bushes. He had been waiting for them to get back, afraid that Tom might do something harmful to Daisy. Gatsby tells Nick that Daisy was driving and that he has decided to take the blame for her. What other decision was possible by a man so deeply in love? He is still afraid to leave and sends Nick to check on Daisy. Nick looks in a window and sees Daisy and Tom sitting opposite each other at the kitchen table, eating cold fried chicken and talking. It is an ordinary domestic scene in sharp contrast to the drama that surrounds them. They aren't happy, but they are not unhappy either. Nick realizes that they have accepted each other again and that Gatsby has lost Daisy irrevocably. She has returned to the protection of Tom's money and influence. He will take care of her and get her through the crisis. Nick goes home and leaves Gatsby "standing there in the moonlight—watching over nothing."

The dream is over.

CHAPTER VIII

Chapter VIII begins a few hours later. Nick has been unable to sleep, and hearing Gatsby come in, he goes over to his friend's house to talk. For the better part of the chapter Nick is alone with Gatsby in his deserted mansion, listening to the story of Gatsby's youth, his courtship of Daisy, and his experiences during the war. The information helps Nick put together the final pieces of the puzzle that is Gatsby. Now that the dream is over, the past is more real to Gatsby than ever. Gatsby hopes that by talking about the Daisy he knew in Louisville in 1917 he can keep the ghost of his dream alive.

All of us have wanted something we couldn't have, something that was beyond our reach. And so, as Gatsby tells Nick about his courtship of Daisy, we can't help but sympathize with him. We can understand how he felt when he entered Daisy's home for the first time and fell in love with everything about her. It was not only Daisy he hungered for, it was her house and her possessions, too. The fact that everybody wanted her merely increased her worth in Gatsby's eyes. He himself was nothing but "a penniless young man without a past." She stood for everything he was not—for everything he wanted to have and to become. And so he "committed himself to the following of a grail," and made marrying Daisy his ultimate goal in life.

NOTE: The grail—or the chalice used by Christ at the Last Supper—is what the knights of the round table were searching for. If they found it, they would be saved. Fitzgerald uses the word *grail* to suggest that for Gatsby, marrying Daisy was a kind of religious quest.

Daisy promised to wait for Gatsby until the war ended. What Gatsby has not bargained for was Daisy's youth and her need for love and the attention of society. She was too frivolous and insecure to stay alone for long, and soon began going out to parties and dances. At one of them, she met Tom Buchanan, who seem safe and strong. She loved Jay, but knew nothing about him—nothing about his past or his practical plans for the future. And he wasn't there. So she married Tom.

The previous chapter took place on the hottest day of the summer. Now it is early morning. Autumn—symbol of change and of the approach of death—is in the air. The gardener informs Gatsby that he will drain the pool, because the falling leaves will clog the pipes. Gatsby asks him to wait a day because he has never used the pool and wants to take a swim.

Nick says good-bye to Gatsby, turns to walk away, then pauses, turns back, and shouts "'They're a rotten crowd. You're worth the whole damn bunch put together.'"

It's a very special moment that reveals to us why the novel is called *The Great Gatsby*. Nick disapproves of Gatsby "from beginning to end"—disapproves of his vulgar materialism; his tasteless pink suits; his "gonnegtion" with Meyer Wolfsheim; his love of a woman as shallow as Daisy; his pathetic efforts to win her back by showing off what he *has* rather than who he *is*. And yet he is not part of the "foul dust." His "incorruptible dream" has something pure and noble about it, which sets him apart from the others. Tom, Daisy, Jordan—they belong to the "rotten crowd" because they are selfish, materialistic, and cruel. They are without spiritual values or compassion. Gatsby, on the surface, seems just as far away from beauty and grace. In reality he is nothing more than a thug. And yet in Nick's eyes—and perhaps in ours—he is "worth the whole damn bunch put together" because of his total dedication to his dream. When the dream is gone, he has nothing left to live for.

Nick takes the train to New York, but he can't work. He keeps thinking about Gatsby. Not even Jordan Baker can get his mind off his friend. She tries to meet him in the city for a date, but Nick turns her down—a fact that will contribute to their eventual break up in the final chapter. Nick is tired of "the whole rotten bunch," and that includes Jordan.

Unable to reach Gatsby by phone, Nick takes an early train back to West Egg. As he passes the valley of ashes, he thinks about Myrtle Wilson's death and tells us what George Wilson was doing from the time of the accident to the present moment. Nick has gotten his information from the Greek Michaelis and from newspaper reports.

Michaelis had sat up all night with George Wilson. At the very moment that Nick and Gatsby were watching the dawn in West Egg, Michaelis and Wilson were looking at the eyes of Dr. T.J. Eckleburg, "which had just emerged, pale and enormous from the dissolving night." To Wilson, the eyes of Dr. Eckleburg are the all-seeing, all-judging eyes of God. Wilson now believes that the car that hit Myrtle was being driven by her lover. He has made up his mind to play God himself and to revenge the murder of his wife. It is simply a matter of finding out who owns the yellow car. His first step is to find Tom Buchanan; Tom drove the car to New York the day before and will know who was driving it back from New York when it hit his wife.

By the time Nick gets to West Egg, Gatsby is lying dead in his pool. The tragedy is complete. Wilson, having found out from Tom where Gatsby lived, had gone to Gatsby's mansion and found him floating on an air mattress in the pool. Wilson had shot Gatsby, then himself.

Nick wonders what Gatsby might have been thinking as he lay on the mattress in the pool just before Wilson's arrival:

> He must have looked up at an unfamiliar sky through frightening leaves and shivered as he found what a grotesque thing a rose is and how

> raw the sunlight was upon the scarcely created grass. A new world, material without being real, where poor ghosts, breathing dreams like air, drifted fortuitously about . . .

One key to understanding this difficult passage is the phrase, "material without being real." What Nick means is that for Gatsby, the world is "material"—it is something he can touch and see and feel—yet it is completely without meaning for him. Without Daisy—without his dream—to sustain him he is like a child who wakes up one day and finds himself in an utterly frightening and unfamiliar world. Gatsby has lived "too long with a single dream"; without it life has become absurd. A rose is beautiful because we feel its beauty, not because it possesses beauty in itself. In the same way, the green light at the end of Daisy's dock was special only because it meant something special to Gatsby. In this new world, which Gatsby encounters a rose is just a rose and a green light is not more than a green light. Gatsby has been forced to grow up, or at least to give up his childlike sense of wonder. Unlike the rest of the rotten crowd, he cannot live without this private vision, and so he is, in a sense, already dead when Wilson shoots him.

CHAPTER IX

Chapter IX covers the period from Gatsby's death to Nick's departure for the Midwest later that autumn. It is a chapter which allows Fitzgerald to tie together loose ends and to sum up the larger significance of the novel in a final poetic passage that has become one of the most famous in American literature.

Nick is still living in the East, but his heart is no longer there. "I found myself on Gatsby's side, and alone," he says. He tries to bring Gatsby's friends together for the funeral, but everyone has conveniently disappeared. Tom and Daisy have gone away, leaving no address. Meyer Wolfsheim does not want to be involved with Gatsby now that the breath of scandal surrounds him. No one visits Gatsby's house now except policemen, photographers, and newspapermen. Finally, on the third day, a telegram arrives from Mr. Henry C. Gatz of Minnesota, Gatsby's father. He has read of his son's death and is on his way. (Is there any religious significance in the fact that the father tries to reach Gatsby three days after his son's death? Gatsby, like Christ, has been scorned by the world and only his father seems to care.) Nick tries to convince Klipspringer, "the boarder," to come to the funeral, but Klipspringer has a social engagement in Westport. When he asks Nick to send his tennis shoes, which he had left at Gatsby's, Nick hangs up on him.

No friends come to the funeral except Owl Eyes, the man who had admired Gatsby's library back in the third chapter. Why he should care enough to come makes for interesting speculation: your ideas are as good as any.

As they stand there in the rain—Nick, Mr. Gatz, Owl Eyes, and a few servants—we cannot help but be appalled by the way his so-called friends have deserted him when he is no longer of any use to them. You can look at their desertion, as Nick surely does, as proof of their moral and spiritual bankruptcy. Or you can argue that Gatsby, in pursuit of a false dream, has brought this fate down on himself.

Gatsby's father, of course, has loved his son all these years and followed his career with special interest. He is proud of his boy and totally unaware of the darker side of his life. He has saved a picture of his son's house, which he apparently takes great pride in showing to others as proof of his son's success. He has also brought along a book, *Hopalong Cassidy,* which Jimmy owned as a boy. On the flyleaf is a daily schedule of exercise, study, sports, "elocution," and work. The schedule, which reads like an excerpt from Ben Franklin's *Almanac,* reminds us how deeply Gatsby believed—even as a boy—in the American dream of success. Like millions of other young Americans, he must have believed that life rewards those who work hard, and that if he only stuck to his plan he could achieve whatever he set out to accomplish. Whether Fitzgerald's novel praises or condemns this dream is something you'll have to determine for yourself.

With the account of Gatsby's funeral, Nick's story comes to an end. In the novel's closing pages, Nick turns in on himself, and talks about his own values and his preparations for a return to the Midwest.

Before he leaves, Nick ends his relationship with Jordan Baker. The scene with Jordan parallels the one at the end of Chapter III where they discuss careless people and bad drivers. In both scenes driving becomes a metaphor for life. Careless drivers stand for those who hurt other people. Jordan is a careless driver, Nick is not. Is this what drew them together and what ultimately pulled them apart? Nick's feelings about Jordan are ambivalent throughout the scene, as they are throughout the book. He is still in love with her, still attracted to her, yet something in him wants to write an end to this chapter in his life. She says she's engaged to another man; he doesn't believe it. We sense that he could probably get her back if he apologized for his behavior on the phone the day of Gatsby's death. But he won't do that.

Nor will he, at first, shake hands with Tom Buchanan when he sees him on Fifth Avenue. Although he blames Tom for Gatsby's death—it was Tom who told Wilson that Gatsby owned the car—he can't really argue with Tom or get mad at him. Why? Because Tom believes that Gatsby was the driver and that his action was "entirely justified." Nick probably realizes that his own moral standards will mean nothing to Tom, and that the only way to deal with his type is to turn around and walk away. Nick at this moment sees Tom and Daisy as careless people who "smashed up things and creatures and then retreated back into their money . . . and let other people clean up the mess they had made." He calls Jordan careless too—a "careless" driver. Nick's decision to leave the East is tied up with his reaction of careless people. He doesn't want to become that way himself. It's uncertain when he finally shakes hands with Tom, whether he has finally learned to accept others who are different from himself, thus getting rid of what Tom calls his "provincial squeamishness"—or whether he is doing only what is proper for a gentleman to do. In any case, he is now rid of Tom and the world he represents, and can return to a world of principles and traditions in the Midwest.

There's no way you can understand Nick's final thoughts without having them in front of you. So, open your books and read Nick's words again. The meaning of the novel is summed up here, and the novel is transformed from a story of a small group of people at a moment of time to a portrait of an entire nation.

It is Nick's last night in West Egg. He has walked over to Gatsby's mansion and erased an obscene word someone has scrawled on the deserted house. He walks down to the beach. As the moon rises and the houses melt away in his imagination, he thinks of what this island must have looked like to the Dutch sailors seeing it for the first time in the sixteenth and seventeenth centuries. It was a new world then—pure, unspoiled. Nick calls it "a fresh green breast of the new world." Nick realizes that men have always been dreamers, but that dreamers cannot simply dream. They must have some object or person to fix their dreams upon. Such was this continent, he thinks, in the early days of the Republic. The *idea* of America as a land of infinite possibilities was so magnificent that man was "face to face for the last time in history with something commensurate to his capacity for wonder." The land—its physical beauty and its apparently limitless horizens—were worthy of the dream.

We have come to call this idea "the American dream." Jefferson, Emerson, Thoreau, and Whitman were only a few of the spokesmen for this dream who saw in America a hope for equality and self-fulfillment. This was Gatsby's dream, too, Nick thinks. For Gatsby the green light at the end of Daisy's dock symbolized the same American dream that drove the Dutch sailors to the New World, the Minutemen to Concord, and Thoreau to Walden Pond. Gatsby believed in the dream, and Nick will always love him for it. But what Gatsby never understood is that the dream was already behind him, "somewhere back in that vast obscurity beyond the city, where the dark fields of the republic rolled on under the night." Unable to find an object or a person commensurate with his capacity for wonder, Gatsby finds Daisy, an unworthy and shallow substitute for the real dream.

NOTE: Nick seems to suggest that America in the 1920s has lost its way—deliberately or inevitably. American has become a shallow, materialistic nation, and the dream for which people fought and about which poets wrote has turned into a cheap and vulgar substitute for the real thing.

Fitzgerald seems to be saying that what keeps Americans going as individuals is the belief in that dream, and so they struggle like Gatsby to attain it. But they are like "boats against the current, borne back ceaselessly into the past." Americans row and row against the current of time, trying to get back to that dream, bearing themselves backward like Gatsby, who believed the past could be repeated, but doomed by the hand of time to failure. Whether Fitzgerald believes Americans can recapture that dream, or whether it's part of their lost childhood—both as individuals and as a nation—is something you'll have to decide for yourself.

The Great Gatsby is not, then, just a book about the 1920s. It is a book about America—its promise, and the betrayal of that promise. Throughout the book Fitzgerald has contrasted Gatsby the dreamer with "the foul dust" that preyed on his dream. The tragedy of Gatsby is that he still dreams the dream, but that he is not wise enough or strong enough to see that Daisy is not worthy of his devotion, of his sacrifice. He cannot step back to see where he has gone wrong. Nick can. Nick loves Gatsby, but he knows what is wrong with Gatsby's dream. And so, his education completed, he returns to the Midwest to begin his own adult life.

A STEP BEYOND

Tests and Answers

TESTS

Test 1

1. Nick Carraway was born _____
   A. in the Northeast B. in the Midwest
   C. in the South

2. The character who first appears "in riding clothes . . . standing with his legs apart on the front porch" is _____
   A. Gatsby B. Tom Buchanan
   C. George Wilson

3. The pretentious expression, "I'm p-paralyzed with happiness," is spoken by _____
   A. Jordan Baker
   B. Daisy Buchanan
   C. Gatsby

4. James Gatz is _____
   A. Daisy's cousin
   B. Gatsby's piano player
   C. Gatsby's real name

5. Nick Carraway recalls a story which implied that Jordan Baker once _____
   A. betrayed a close friend
   B. stole some money
   C. cheated at golf

6. Gatsby shows a police officer _____
   A. a fifty dollar bill
   B. a Christmas card from the police commissioner

C. the damage done to the front fender of his car

7. The character who hangs up the phone in Nick's ear "with a sharp click" is _____
A. Gatsby B. Tom Buchanan
C. Jordan Baker

8. When Nick tells Gatsby, "You can't repeat the past," Gatsby replies _____
A. "Of course you can."
B. "After all I've done? That's nonsense."
C. "I'd never thought of that before, Old Sport."

9. Doctor T.J. Eckleburg becomes a symbol of _____
A. Gatsby's "romantic readiness"
B. Nick's friendship for Gatsby
C. the lack of morals prevalent in the East

10. Myrtle Wilson's nose is broken by _____
A. Gatsby B. Tom Buchanan
C. George Wilson

11. Is Gatsby a "hero?" Discuss.

12. Describe Fitzgerald's attitude toward money in *The Great Gatsby*.

13. Discuss Nick Carraway as Narrator and Character.

14. Analyze Fitzgerald's use of setting as "moral geography."

15. Select one of the major symbols of the novel and show how Fitzgerald uses it.

Test 2

1. The expression "and the holocaust was complete" refers to _____
A. Myrtle's death

B. George Wilson's death
C. Gatsby's death

2. Nick left his home to come to New York in an effort to ____
A. make money B. meet new people
C. locate Gatsby

3. The character who has "one of those rare smiles with a quality of eternal reassurance in it, that you may come across four or five times in life" is ____
A. Daisy Buchanan B. Gatsby
C. Jordan Baker

4. The character who, according to Gatsby, "fixed the world series" is ____
A. Wolfsheim B. Klipspringer
C. Owl Eyes

5. Apparently, most of Gatsby's money has come from ____
A. drug sales B. bootlegging
C. bond investments

6. When Myrtle Wilson is killed, the car that hit her was driven by ____
A. Gatsby B. Daisy C. Tom

7. "The promise of a decade of loneliness" is sensed by ____
A. Nick B. Gatsby C. Dan Cody

8. The most significant *change* in Daisy's life since before the war is that she now ____
A. has a child B. loves Gatsby
C. likes having money

9. "That ashen, fantastic figure gliding toward him through the amorphous trees" is ____
A. George Wilson B. Gatsby
C. Tom Buchanan

10. A symbol of the human capacity for hope is _____
    A. Gatsby's immense mansion
    B. the green light at the end of Daisy's dock
    C. Owl Eyes

11. Compare and contrast *The Great Gatsby* and Conrad's *Heart of Darkness.*

12. Analyze the influence of T. S. Eliot's "The Waste Land" on *The Great Gatsby.*

13. Discuss Fitzgerald's handling of time in *The Great Gatsby.*

14. Show how Gatsby and Nick are really the two sides of Fitzgerald.

15. Describe how *The Great Gatsby* is a commentary on the American Dream.

ANSWERS

Test 1

1. B 2. B 3. B 4. C 5. C 6. B

7. C 8. A 9. C 10. B

11. Everyone wants to admire someone. Do you admire Gatsby? Is he a hero to you? If so, why? If not, why not? This essay gives you a wonderful opportunity to take sides. From one point of view, Gatsby is a crook, a bootlegger, a vulgar materialist. From another point of view, he is a dreamer, faithful to his dream to the very end. Nick sees him as "great," despite the fact that Gatsby stands for many things that Nick doesn't believe in.

To write this essay you will want to look with particular care at those passages where Nick talks about Gatsby—both near the middle of Chapter VIII, and in the closing pages of the novel. If you think that Gatsby is *not* a hero, you will want to pay special attention to Meyer Wolfsheim and to

Gatsby's association with him. Look at the many strange phone calls from Philadelphia and Chicago and at Tom's thoughts in Chapter VII on what Wolfsheim and Gatsby did to Walter Chase.

For further details see the section on "Jay Gatsby" in The Characters.

12. Most of us, like Fitzgerald, have ambivalent feelings about money. We want it, we are excited by it, but we don't want it to dominate our lives. What do you think Fitzgerald's attitude toward money is in this novel? Does he treat all the rich characters in the same way? Is money itself good or evil, or does it depend on who is using it and for what purpose? These are all questions an essay might explore.

You will want to look at the description of Tom and Daisy's house in Chapter I and of Gatsby's house in Chapter III. Nick's comment about Tom and Daisy's money near the end of the final chapter is helpful, as is Nick's description of Tom as a character in Chapter I. Look at the scene in Chapter V where Gatsby shows off his possessions to Daisy. Why does Daisy cry in his shirts? What does this say about her attitude toward money and about things money can buy?

There is no easy answer to this question, so don't feel that any one answer is right. Fitzgerald, as you read in The Author and His Times, said that he could hold two contradictory views at the same time. Perhaps that is what you think he does in this book?

13. This is a good essay question for those who enjoy debating with the critics. Most readers find Nick what is called a "reliable narrator." They share his views and read the novel from his point of view. A few critics disagree. They say Nick is immature and should be more critical of Gatsby than he is. They argue that Nick is too sentimental about Gatsby, and that it would be very dangerous for *us* to adopt the same attitude that Nick adopts.

In writing this essay, you will want to understand clearly Nick's attitudes toward this Eastern world and the characters who live in it. Nick expresses his attitudes mainly in the first and last chapters. Once you have explored his point of view, you should be prepared to argue either that Fitzgerald shares Nick's views and wants us to share them, too; or that we as readers are being asked to be more mature and realistic than Nick is. Gary Scrimgeour's essay "Against *The Great Gatsby*," (see The Critics section) makes a good case against Nick, if you're looking for some help with your argument.

14. We have discussed this issue at length both in the section on setting and in the places in the scene-by-scene discussion where each of the settings is introduced for the first time. You will particularly want to review the opening three chapters where East Egg, West Egg, the valley of ashes, and New York City are each introduced for the first time. Ask yourself what values is each place associated with. Is Fitzgerald supporting one set of values against the others? If so, with which of the places are we most asked to identify? Why? Write about the fact that all of the characters are originally from the Midwest—an important factor in this equation of place with values. In writing your essay, you may want to compare the locations in this novel with locations in your own community.

15. Be sure you know what a symbol is before you start. Hugh Holman's *A Handbook to Literature* is very helpful. Then select the symbol you want to write about and go through the novel, noting each place it is mentioned. The green light is mentioned at the end of Chapter I, the middle of Chapter V, and on the last page of the novel. The eyes of Dr. T. J. Eckleburg are described in detail at the beginning of Chapter II. They are also an important part of Michaelis' description of George Wilson's state of mind in Chapter VIII.

Remember as you write that symbols don't mean just one thing. Symbols are pointers that merely *suggest* other things beyond themselves.

Test 2

1. B **2.** A **3.** B **4.** A **5.** B **6.** B

7. A **8.** A **9.** A **10.** B

11. This is a particularly good essay topic if you have already studied *Heart of Darkness*. Both novels are short, compact, intense. In each case, an inexperienced young man who is the narrator (Nick in Fitzgerald's novel, Marlow in Conrad's) goes on a journey and meets an extraordinary character who has a profound influence on the young man's life. In each case the young man comes to admire the extraordinary character, even though that character is someone the world might not admire. The heroes (Gatsby and Kurtz) die, and the young narrators are moved by those deaths to tell their stories. Fitzgerald modeled *The Great Gatsby* on *Heart of Darkness*, and a study of the two books together would be most rewarding.

If the essay is a shorter one, then merely compare and contrast Nick and Marlow or Gatsby and Kurtz.

12. If you have read Eliot's famous poem, published in 1922, you cannot help but be struck by some of the ways in which Fitzgerald learned from Eliot. Eliot's poem is full of images of barrenness, dryness, and sterility. His "Waste Land" is a desert land, thirsty for the water of spiritual rebirth. In Eliot's world the characters are shallow, without lasting values, without deep feelings. Fitzgerald's characters, even the minor ones who show up at Gatsby's parties, suffer from the same emptiness, symbolized by "dust." Fitzgerald's valley of ashes is a symbol that may have been inspired directly by Eliot's masterpiece. Both Eliot and Fitzgerald were young men who became spokesmen for their generation. Many young men in the 1920s who read "The Waste Land" said that the poem expressed their own feelings about life; many said the same about Fitzgerald's work.

13. How do we get to know people? We meet them, become interested in them, start a friendship perhaps, and then take an interest in their past lives. We get to know Gatsby in the same way. In the first three chapters Fitzgerald explores the present—the summer of 1922. In Chapters IV, VI, and VIII he takes us into the world of Gatsby's past. Gatsby is a kind of mystery to be solved, and we are given more and more clues as we go along. Our last piece of information about Gatsby's past does not come until Chapter IX, only pages before the end of the book. Discuss whether you find this movement back and forth from past to present more interesting than being told a story chronologically. (For more details, read comments on Form and Structure.)

14. Fitzgerald often said that he had a romantic side that made him throw himself passionately into parties, and into other intense experiences with Zelda. That side didn't know when to say "no," and it often drove Fitzgerald into situations that were dangerous and destructive. The other side of Fitzgerald was hard working, disciplined. This side of him wanted to be a famous writer and knew how much self-restraint and hard work were required to do the job well. You can argue in your paper that these two sides of Fitzgerald are captured in turn, by Nick and Gatsby.

It will help you to reread the section of this guide called The Author and His Times, and to read one of the fine Fitzgerald biographies by Arthur Mizener or Andrew Turnbull. You may want to take your essay a step afield by considering Gatsby and Nick as the two sides of any human being including yourself.

15. This subject has been treated frequently throughout this guidebook. See especially the comments under Themes, in the section called Other Elements. Marius Bewley's excellent essay, "Scott Fitzgerald's Criticism of America," is also very helpful (see The Critics section). You will need to think about what the phrase "the American dream" means and whether or not it means the same thing as "the American dream of success." If it is "American" for a young man without money or family background to want to make it big, what is wrong with Gatsby's dream?

Fitzgerald hints at an answer to this and related questions in the extraordinary passage on the final page of the novel (see commentary on Chapter IX). You will have to decide finally whether you think Fitzgerald is criticizing the American dream itself or just the form that the dream is taking during the 1920s.

Term Paper Ideas

1. Who is the central character of *The Great Gatsby*, Nick or Gatsby? Why?

2. Examine Fitzgerald's use of Nick as narrator of the story. What are the advantages and/or problems of telling the story in this way?

3. Examine Nick's values. How are these similar to or different from the values of the other characters?

4. Analyze Jay Gatsby. What makes him "great"?

5. Analyze Gatsby's dream. What does he believe in? Is his dream worthwhile?

6. Analyze Nick's attitude toward Gatsby's dream. Do you think Nick is being too sentimental?

7. What is meant by the phrase "the American dream"? How is *Gatsby* a novel about the American dream?

8. Study Gatsby's past: his family background, his education under Dan Cody, his meeting with Daisy in Louisville in 1917. How does our knowledge of his past help us to understand who he really is?

9. Analyze the symbolism of the green light at the end of Daisy's dock.

10. Anaylze the symbolism of the eyes of Dr. T.J. Eckleburg.

11. Write an essay on the use of color symbolism in the novel, especially the colors white and yellow.

12. Examine the symbolic use of names in the novel. Are the names simply realistic or do they stand for something beyond themselves?

13. Examine the valley of ashes as a symbolic setting in the novel. How is it related to T. S. Eliot's "Waste Land"?

14. Examine East Egg, especially the home of Tom and Daisy Buchanan, as a "moral" setting. What values of the Buchanans are mirrored in their life-style?

15. Examine the world of West Egg, especially Gatsby's mansion. How is it different from East Egg. Why? What does it represent?

16. Examine New York City as a setting, especially through the two parties which occur in New York in Chapters II and VII.

17. Examine Tom Buchanan as a character. Is he sympathetic? If not, why? How does he symbolize the world of the very rich?

18. Examine Jordan Baker as a character, looking at her name, her honesty or dishonesty, her athletic career, her relationship with Nick.

19. Examine Myrtle Wilson as a character. What makes us sympathetic to her? How is she in some ways like Gatsby?

20. Look closely at the world of Gatsby's parties and the people who come to them. Who are they and how do they feel about Gatsby?

21. Analyze the role of Meyer Wolfsheim in the novel. He is based on Arnold Rothstein ("the man who fixed the 1919 World Series"). You may wish to do some research on Rothstein.

22. Do some reading on prohibition in the 1920s. How did the bootlegging business develop and who controlled it? How does our knowledge of this affect our understanding of Gatsby?

23. Scott and Zelda Fitzgerald lived in Great Neck, Long Island, during the early 1920s and gave and went to parties similar to Gatsby's. Do some reading on Scott and Zelda in Mizener or Turnbull and analyze the similarities and/or differences between the two worlds—Fitzgerald's and Gatsby's.

24. Fitzgerald admitted that Gatsby started out as a particular person and ended up as part of himself. How is Fitzgerald like Gatsby? What aspects of himself does Fitzgerald seem to be dramatizing in Gatsby?

25. Fitzgerald put another part of himself in Nick Carraway. How would you describe this aspect of Fitzgerald?

26. Compare and contrast Gatsby and Carraway as parts of Fitzgerald or as parts of yourself.

27. What is meant by the term, "The Jazz Age"? How is *The Great Gatsby* a portrait of the times?

28. What do you think of the morality of the characters? Is Fitzgerald passing judgment on them? Are we being asked to?

29. Compare and contrast the parties in the first three chapters (the one at Tom and Daisy's, the one in New York, and the one at Gatsby's). What do we learn from an analysis of these three worlds?

30. Do a close analysis of the scenes in Chapter V where Gatsby meets Daisy for the first time and takes her to see his house and his possessions. Does this scene increase your sympathy for Gatsby?

31. Do a close analysis of the two parties at Gatsby's house (Chapters II and VI). How are they similar? How different? Is the difference important in the development of the novel's themes?

32. Do a close analysis of the last page of the novel. What is Fitzgerald saying about the past? About American history?

33. Fitzgerald first thought of calling *The Great Gatsby* "Trimalchio in West Egg" or "Trimalchio." Who is Trimalchio? (See Glossary.) Compare and contrast Trimalchio and Gatsby.

34. The narrative technique of *Gatsby* is modeled on Joseph Conrad's *Heart of Darkness.* Compare and contrast the two works, thematically and stylistically.

35. Compare and contrast Nick Carraway with Marlow in Conrad's *Heart of Darkness.*

36. Compare and contrast Gatsby with Kurtz in Conrad's *Heart of Darkness.*

37. Read the sections in Wayne C. Booth's *The Rhetoric of Fiction* on the difference between reliable and unreliable narrators. Would you consider Nick Carraway to be reliable?

38. Analyze Fitzgerald's style in *Gatsby.* What do you think he is best at? Dialogue? Description? Narration of events? Reflection?

39 Examine *The Great Gatsby* as a tragedy. Who is the tragic hero?

40. Examine Daisy Buchanan as a character. What parallels do you see between her and Zelda Fitzgerald?

41. Look at the people who attend Gatsby's funeral. Who are they? Who does not come? What comment is Fitzgerald making through this contrast?

42. There is a lot of talk about carelessness in the novel. What does Fitzgerald mean by "carelessness"? Who is called careless and why?

43. Is *Gatsby* just a book for rich people? If you are poor or black or Hispanic, how do you react to this book? What does it say to you about America?

44. Is *Gatsby* relevant to the late 20th century? If so, how?

45. Compare Rudolph Miller in the story "Absolution" with Jay Gatsby. Fitzgerald originally intended to use "Absolution" as a preface to *Gatsby*. What parallels do you see?

46. Compare Dexter Green in the story "Winter Dreams" with Jay Gatsby. What relationships do you see between the characters?

47. As a college or high school student, you go to parties and seek out members of the opposite sex in hopes of winning them. Does Gatsby's seeking out of Daisy correspond to this aspect of your life?

48. Analyze the East and the Midwest as symbols of different morals and life-styles in the novel. Does the contrast still hold?

49. The novel centers on three sexual relationships—Gatsby–Daisy, Tom–Myrtle, Nick–Jordan. Write an essay comparing and contrasting these three affairs. Do you feel the same about all of them?

50. Fitzgerald himself said the greatest flaw of the novel was his failure to develop the relationship between Gatsby and Daisy after their reunion in West Egg. Do you agree? What other flaws are there?

Further Reading

CRITICAL WORKS

Much has been written about F. Scott Fitzgerald and about *The Great Gatsby* in particular. The list that follows includes some of the most important works.

Biographies

Donaldson, Scott. *Fool for Love*. New York: Congdon & Weed, 1983

Milford, Nancy. *Zelda*. New York: Harper & Row, 1970.

Mizener, Arthur. *The Far Side of Paradise*. Boston: Houghton Mifflin, 1951.

Turnbull, Andrew. *Scott Fitzgerald*. New York: Scribner's, 1962.

Critical Studies—Books

Hoffman, Frederick J., ed. *The Great Gatsby: A Study*. New York: Scribner's, 1962.

______. *The Twenties*. New York: Viking Press, 1955.

Kazin, Alfred. *F. Scott Fitzgerald: The Man and His Work*. Cleveland: World, 1951.

Lockridge, Ernest H., ed. *Twentieth Century Interpretations of The Great Gatsby*. Englewood Cliffs: Prentice-Hall, 1968.

Miller, James E., Jr. *The Fictional Technique of Scott Fitzgerald*. The Hague: M. Nijhoff, 1957

______. *F. Scott Fitzgerald: His Art and His Technique*. New York: New York University Press, 1964.

Mizener, Arthur F., ed. *F. Scott Fitzgerald: A Collection of Critical Essays*. Englewood Cliffs: Prentice-Hall, 1963.

Perosa, Sergio. *The Art of F. Scott Fitzgerald*. Ann Arbor: University of Michigan Press, 1965.

Piper, Henry Dan. *F. Scott Fitzgerald: A Critical Portrait*. New York: Holt, 1965.

Trilling, Lionel. "F. Scott Fitzgerald" in *The Liberal Imagination*. Garden City: Doubleday, 1950.

Critical Studies—Articles

Bewley, Marius. "Scott Fitzgerald's Criticism of America." *Sewanee Review* 62 (Spring, 1954), 223–46.

Bicknell, John W. "The Wasteland of F. Scott Fitzgerald." *Virginia Quarterly Review*, 30 (Autumn; 1954), 556–72.

Cowley, Malcolm. "Third Act and Epilogue." *The New Yorker* (June 30, 1945).

Dyson, A.E. " 'The Great Gatsby': 36 Years After." *Modern Fiction Studies*, 7 (Spring, 1962), 162–67.

Fussell, Edwin. "Fitzgerald's Brave New World." *English Literary History*, 19 (December, 1952), 291–306.

Hanzo, Thomas A. "The Theme and the Narrator of 'The Great Gatsby.'" *Modern Fiction Studies*, 2 (Winter, 1956–57), 183–190.

Hemingway, Ernest. "Scott Fitzgerald" and "Hawks Do Not Share" in *A Moveable Feast* (New York: Charles Scribner's Sons, 1964), 145–191.

Hindus, Milton. "The Eyes of Dr. T.J. Eckleburg." *Boston University Studies in English*, 3 (Spring, 1957), 22–31.

Ornstein, Robert. "Scott Fitzgerald's Fable of East and West." *College English*, 18 (December, 1956), 139–43.

Schneider, Daniel J. "Color-Symbolism in The Great Gatsby." *The University Review*, 31 (1964), 13–18.

Scrimgeour, Gary J. "Against *The Great Gatsby*." *Criticism*, 8 (Winter, 1966), 75–86.

Stallman, Robert W. "Conrad and *The Great Gatsby*." *Twentieth Century Literature* 1 (April, 1955), 5–12.

Thale, Jerome. "The Narrator as Hero." *Twentieth Century Literature*, 3 (July, 1957), 69–73.

AUTHOR'S OTHER WORKS

This Side of Paradise (novel), 1920
Flappers and Philosophers (short stories), 1920
The Beautiful and Damned (novel), 1921
Tales of the Jazz Age (stories), 1922
All the Sad Young Men (stories), 1926
Tender is the Night (novel), 1934
Taps at Reveille (stories), 1935
The Last Tycoon (unfinished novel), ed. Edmund Wilson, 1941
The Crack-Up (essays), ed. Edmund Wilson, 1945
The Stories of F. Scott Fitzgerald. A Selection of 28 Stories, ed. Malcolm Cowley, 1951
Afternoon of an Author (uncollected stories and essays), ed. Arthur Mizener, 1957
The Letters of F. Scott Fitzgerald, ed. Andrew Turnbull, 1963
Letters to His Daughter, ed. Andrew Turnbull, 1965

Glossary

The Glossary is limited to proper nouns, the meaning of which might not be clear in the context of the novel. Symbolic terms such as *grail* or *incarnation* are explained in the chapter-by-chapter analysis.

"Ain't We Got Fun" A very popular song of the day, Klipspringer sings it to Gatsby and Daisy in Chapter VI.

Belasco David Belasco (1853–1931) was a very successful American actor, producer, playwright, and theater manager. Owl Eyes thinks of Gatsby as a "regular Belasco," because of his magnificent library and real books.

James J. Hill American railroad tycoon and financier (1838–1916); one of many rich Americans referred to in the novel.

Kaiser Wilhelm The Emperor of Germany in 1914 at the outbreak of World War I. Gatsby is suspected of being a nephew of Kaiser Wilhelm.

Kant Immanuel Kant (1724–1804) was famous German philosopher who stared at a church steeple to help his concentration. Nick, in Chapter V, stares at Gatsby's house, "like Kant at his church steeple."

Lake Forest A suburb of Chicago where very rich and socially prestigious families live. Tom Buchanan comes East with a string of polo ponies from Lake Forest.

Midas . . . Morgan . . . Maecenas The first was the legendary king who was granted his wish that everything he touch change to gold. "Morgan" refers to J. Pierpont Morgan (1837–1913), the famous New York financier. "Maecenas" was a wealthy Etruscan patron of the Roman poets Horace and Virgil. All three are examples of Fitzgerald's fascination with wealth and the very wealthy.

Montenegro Once a small country on the Adriatic Sea, now part of Yugoslavia. Gatsby says he has a medal from "little Montenegro."

New Haven The city in Connecticut where Yale University is located. "New Haven" in this novel means Yale, where Tom and Nick went to college.

Oxford Oxford University in England. Meyer Wolfsheim refers to it mistakenly as "Oggsford College." Oxford is not a college, but a university made up of a collection of colleges.

Plaza Hotel The famous hotel in New York City at the corner of Fifth Avenue and Central Park South. You can still take carriage rides from the Plaza today (see Chapter IV).

Rockefeller John D. Rockefeller (1839–1937) was an industrialist and philanthropist who founded the Standard Oil Company. He was perhaps the ultimate symbol of wealth in the United States.

"Sheik of Araby" Another popular song of the day overheard by Nick and Jordan in New York.

Tostoff Vladimir Tostoff's *Jazz History of the World* is an imaginary composition by an imaginary composer. The jazz orchestra plays it for the guests at Gatsby's party in Chapter III. It's self-important title is Fitzgerald's cynical comment on how jazz tried to present itself as a serious rival to classical music during the '20s.

Trimalchio Central character of the *Satyricon* by Petronius. Trimalchio is a vulgar, self-made millionaire whose brief and meteoric rise to the top parallels Gatsby's brief career. Fitzgerald thought of calling the novel, "Trimalchio in West Egg."

Von Hindenburg German general, chief of staff in World War I, later president of the Weimar Republic. Some say Gatsby worked for von Hindenberg—another example of the Gatsby myth.

World Series of 1919 The famous "Black Sox" scandal in which the Chicago White Sox deliberately lost the World Series to the Cincinnati Reds, a much weaker team, in order to make money for themselves. The arrangements were made through a group of gamblers, the key figure of which was Arnold Rothstein, the model for Meyer Wolfsheim in *Gatsby*. (See Chapter IV.)

The Critics

A letter to Fitzgerald from his editor, November 20, 1924

I think you have every kind of right to be proud of this book. It is an extraordinary book, suggestive of all sorts of thoughts and moods. You adopted exactly the right method of telling it, that of employing a narrator who is more of a spectator than an actor: this puts the reader upon a point of observation on a higher level than that on which the characters stand and at a distance that gives perspective. In no other way could your irony have been so immensely effective, nor the reader have been enabled so strongly to feel at times the strangeness of human circumstance in a vast heedless universe. In the eyes of Dr. Eckleburg various readers will see different significances; but their presence gives a superb touch to the whole thing: great unblinking eyes, expressionless, looking down upon the human scene. It's magnificent!

Maxwell Perkins, *Editor to Author: The Letters of Maxwell E. Perkins*, 1950

Fitzgerald's dream: a parallel to Gatsby

When I was your age I lived with a great dream. The dream grew and I learned how to speak of it and make people listen. Then the dream divided one day when I decided to marry your mother after all, even though I knew she was spoiled and meant no good to me. I was sorry immediately I had married her, but being patient in those days, made the best of it and got to love her in another way. You came along and for a long time we made quite a lot of happiness out of our lives. But I was a man divided—she wanted me to work too much for her and not enough for my dream. She realized too late that work was dignity, and the only dignity, and tried to atone for it by working herself, but it was too late and she broke and is broken forever.

Scott Fitzgerald, "Letter to His Daughter," July 7, 1938 from *Letters to His Daughter*, 1965

Fitzgerald's double vision

He cultivated a sort of double vision. He was continually trying to present the glitter of life in the Princeton eating clubs, on the Riviera, on the North Shore of Long Island, and in the Hollywood studios; he surrounded his characters with a mist of admiration and simultaneously he drove the mist away. . . . He regarded himself as a pauper living among millionaires . . . a sullen peasant among the nobility, and he said that his point of vantage "was the dividing line between two generations," prewar and postwar. It was this habit of keeping a double point of view that distinguished his work. There were popular and serious novelists in his time, but there was something of a gulf between them; Fitzgerald was one of the very few popular writers who were also serious artists.

Malcolm Cowley, "Third Act and Epilogue," *The New Yorker*, 1945

Fitzgerald's artistic method in *Gatsby*

. . . the characters are not "developed": the wealthy and brutal Tom Buchanan haunted by his "scientific" vision of the doom of civilization, the vaguely guilty, vaguely homosexual Jordan Baker, the dim Wolfsheim, who fixed the World Series of 1919, are treated, we might say, as if they were ideographs, a method of economy that is reinforced by the ideographic use of that is made of the Washington Heights flat, the terrible "valley of ashes" seen from the Long Island Railroad, Gatsby's incoherent parties, and the huge sordid eyes of the oculist's advertising sign. (It is a technique which gives the novel an affinity with *The Waste Land*, between whose author and Fitzgerald there existed a reciprocal admiration.) Gatsby himself, once stated, grows only in the understanding of the narrator. He is allowed to say very little in his own person. Indeed, apart from the famous "Her voice is full of money," he says only one memorable thing, but that remark is overwhelming in its intellectual audacity: when he is forced to admit that his lost Daisy did perhaps love her husband, he says, "In any case it was just personal." With that sentence he achieves an insane greatness, convincing us that he really is a Platonic conception of himself, really some sort of Son of God.

Lionel Trilling, "F. Scott Fitzgerald,"
The Liberal Imagination, 1950

The Great Gatsby and the American dream

The Great Gatsby is an exploration of the American dream as it exists in a corrupt period, and it is an attempt to determine that concealed boundary that divides the reality from the illusions. The illusions seem more real than the reality itself. Embodied in the subordinate characters in the novel, they threaten to invade the whole of the picture. On the other hand, the reality is embodied in Gatsby; and as opposed to the hard, tangible illusions, the reality is a thing of the spirit, a promise rather than the possession of a vision, a faith in the half-glimpsed, but hardly understood possibilities of life.

Marius Bewley, "Scott Fitzgerald's
Criticism of America," 1954

The symbolism of East and West

Fitzgerald's dichotomy of East and West has the poetic truth of James's antithesis of provincial American virtue and refined European sensibility. Like *The Portrait of a Lady* and *The Ambassadors*, *Gatsby* is a story of "displaced persons" who have journeyed eastward in search of a larger experience of life. To James this reverse migration from the New to the Old World has in itself no special significance. To Fitzgerald, however, the lure of the East represents a profound displacement of the American dream, a turning back upon itself of the historic pilgrimage towards the frontier which had, in fact, created and sustained that dream.

Robert Ornstein, "Scott Fitzgerald's
Fable of East and West," 1957

Color symbolism in *The Great Gatsby*: Daisy

The white Daisy embodies the vision which Gatsby (who, like Lord Jim, usually wears white suits) seeks to embrace—but which Nick, who discovers the corrupt admixture of dream and reality, rejects in rejecting Jordan. For, except in Gatsby's extravagant imagination, the white does not exist pure: it is invariably stained by the money, the yellow. Daisy is the white flower—with the golden center. If in her virginal beauty she "dressed in white and had a little white roadster," she is, Nick realizes, "high in a white palace the king's daughter, the golden girl." "Her voice is like money"; she carries a "little gold pencil"; when she visits Gatsby there are "two rows of brass buttons on her dress."

Daniel J. Schneider, "Color-Symbolism in *The Great Gatsby*," 1964

An attack on Nick as a character

Carraway's distinctiveness as a character is that he fails to learn anything from his story, that he can continue to blind himself even after his privileged overview of Gatsby's fate. . . . He refuses to admit that his alliance with Gatsby, his admiration for the man, results from their sharing the same weakness. . . . He has learned nothing. His failure to come to any self-knowledge makes him like the person who blames the stone for stubbing his toe. It seems inevitable that he will repeat the same mistakes as soon as the feeling that "temporarily closed out my interest in the abortive sorrows and short-winded elations of men" has departed. . . . Had Carraway been defeated by the impersonal forces of an evil world in which he was an ineffectual innocent, his very existence—temporary or not—would lighten the picture. But his defeat is caused by something that lies within himself: his own lack of fibre, his own willingness to deny reality, his own substitution of dreams for knowledge of self and the world, his own sharing in the very vices of which his fellow men stand accused.

Gary J. Scrimgeour, "Against The Great Gatsby," 1966

Klett LernTraining®

Einfach bessere Noten

Die Reihen, die allen Bedürfnissen gerecht werden, im Überblick

1. Training – **Nachhilfe aus dem Buch**

2. Die kleinen Lerndrachen – **Training für alle Grundschüler**

3. PC-Kombi-Training – **die Fitness-Programme: Kombination aus Lernbuch und Übungssoftware**

4. Lektürehilfen – **Durchblick bei der Lektüre**

5. Abiturwissen – **das geballte Wissen fürs Abi**

6. Abi-Training – **fit fürs Abi**

7. PC-Kurswissen – **pures Abi–Wissen aus dem Computer**

**Klett LernTraining im Internet:
www.klett-verlag.de/klett-lerntraining**

**Das Lernhits-Gesamtverzeichnis:
in Ihrer Buchhandlung oder
direkt bei Ernst Klett Verlag,
Postfach 10 60 16, 70049 Stuttgart**